THE LOVE OF
BASEBALL

Publications International, Ltd.

Contributing writers: Paul Adomites, Robert Cassidy, Bruce Herman,
Dan Schlossberg, and Saul Wisnia

Factual verification by Bruce Herman and Marty Strasen.

Pages 29, 59, 105, 114, 117, 147, and 215: Reprinted with permission from *Baseball Digest*.

All Yogi Berra quotes contained in this text are reprinted with permission from
LTD Enterprises, Inc., Little Falls, NJ.

Louis Weber, CEO
Publications International, Ltd.
7373 North Cicero Avenue
Lincolnwood, Illinois 60712

Permission is never granted for commercial purposes.

Manufactured in China.

8 7 6 5 4 3 2 1

ISBN-13: 978-1-4127-1131-9
ISBN-10: 1-4127-1131-2

Library of Congress Control Number: 2004115108

Contents

CHAPTER ONE

Busting Fences *&*
Chasing Flies

"Say this much for baseball—it is beyond question

the *greatest conversation piece*

ever invented in America."

—BRUCE CATTON,
FASCINATING BASEBALL FACTS

The Glorified Game

With the notable exceptions of war and romance, baseball seems to have been glorified in film, television, books, and song more than any other American pastime. The highs and lows of life as defined in a single at-bat moved masses in the celebrated Ernest Lawrence Thayer poem, "Casey at the Bat." While the line "there is no joy in Mudville" has become a familiar way of describing failure, hordes of fans have seen fit to rewrite the ending so the hero doesn't strike out. The song "Take Me Out to the Ballgame" has been subject to more renditions and revisions than anything this side of "Happy Birthday," while millions of folks who don't know one double-play combo from another know the rhythmic flow of the words "Tinker to Evers to Chance."

When musicians Simon and Garfunkel sought to capture the lost innocence of Vietnam-era Americans, all it took was one line in their 1967 hit "Mrs. Robinson": "Where have you gone, Joe DiMaggio? Our nation turns its lonely eyes to you." Beginning with Thomas Edison's 1898 glimpse of two amateur clubs battling it out in "The Ball Game," baseball has been the subject of hundreds of screen adaptations. If not always great art, the results are at least resoundingly American—leaving fans to hope that fathers and sons will play catch, just like Kevin Costner and his dad in *Field of Dreams*.

The Great *Home Run* Chase

In 1998 St. Louis' Mark McGwire and the Cubs' Sammy Sosa thrilled the nation with their assault on baseball's season home run record. With its spirit of competitive camaraderie, the race was more than just a pursuit of numbers; it captured imaginations nationwide. Big Mac surpassed Roger Maris's major-league mark with his 62nd homer on

"I can't believe I did it," McGwire said. "Can you?"

September 8. Slammin' Sammy continued the drama by tying McGwire at 66. But Mac distanced himself on the final weekend, finishing with the then-unfathomable total of 70.

"All I want out of life is that when I walk down the street, people will say, 'There goes the greatest hitter who ever lived.'"

—TED WILLIAMS

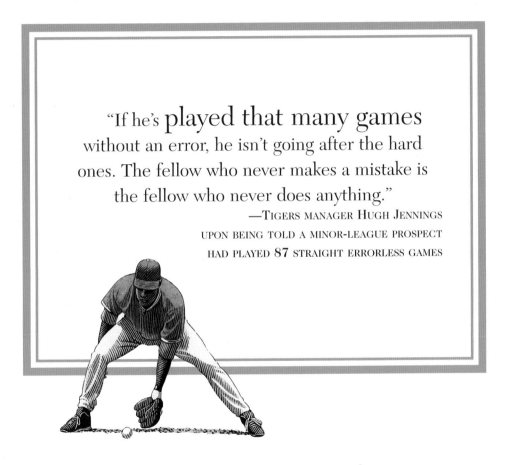

"If he's played that many games without an error, he isn't going after the hard ones. The fellow who never makes a mistake is the fellow who never does anything."

—TIGERS MANAGER HUGH JENNINGS
UPON BEING TOLD A MINOR-LEAGUE PROSPECT
HAD PLAYED 87 STRAIGHT ERRORLESS GAMES

Fenway Park, Boston

In no place on Earth is the purity of the game and the fan's honest experience of it so powerful as in Boston's Fenway Park. Dating back more than 90 years, the legendary park hosted the 1912 World Series, Babe Ruth's first big-league game, and the immortal feats of Ted Williams. Boston's deeply knowledgeable fans, between bites of a Fenway Frank, will tell you all about it. The famed "Green Monster," which Carlton Fisk slayed in the 1975 World Series, stands like a national monument in left field.

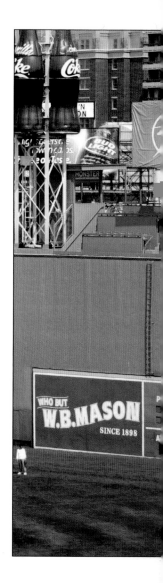

World Series *Perfection*

With the 1956 World Series tied at two games apiece, the Yankees needed some 1–2–3 innings from Don Larsen in the pivotal Game 5 against Brooklyn. He responded with nine of them, throwing the only perfect game—and, in fact, the only no-hitter—in postseason history. After Larsen struck out Dale Mitchell to end the game, catcher Yogi Berra leapt into his pitcher's arms in jubilation. Afterward, a reporter asked, "Is that the best game you ever pitched?"

"Just before I threw the last pitch to Mitchell, I said to myself, *'Well, here goes nothing.'*"
—DON LARSEN

Mantle's Mammoth Blast

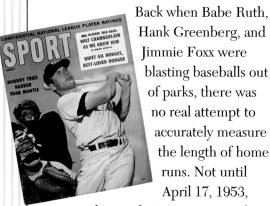

Back when Babe Ruth, Hank Greenberg, and Jimmie Foxx were blasting baseballs out of parks, there was no real attempt to accurately measure the length of home runs. Not until April 17, 1953, were the words "tape-measure shot" ever uttered in reference to a homer. That afternoon, in Washington's Griffith Stadium, 20-year-old Yankee center fielder Mickey Mantle added the expression to baseball's vernacular with one swing of his bat.

Facing Senators lefty Chuck Stobbs in the top of the fifth inning, the switch-hitting Mantle took position on the right side of the plate and dug in. Not offering at the first pitch, he met the second dead-on with a tremendous cut that launched the ball on a fast climb to left-center field. It cleared the bleachers, nicked off the upper-side of a beer sign atop an old football scoreboard (approximately 460 feet from home plate), then disappeared from view.

The tiny crowd of 4,206 in the stadium was stunned, but one man acted fast. Running out of the press box into the streets behind left field, Yankee PR director Arthur "Red" Patterson saw a 10-year-old kid with the ball and asked where he found it. Escorted to a yard on an adjacent street, Patterson paced off 105 feet from the base of the wall behind the bleachers. The final estimated distance of 565 feet was reported in the papers the next day—and the tape-measure homer was born.

"I honestly feel that it would be best for the country to keep baseball going… if 300 teams use 5,000 or 6,000 players, these players are a definite asset to at least 20,000,000 of their fellow citizens—and that in my judgment is thoroughly worthwhile."

—President Franklin Delano Roosevelt's "green light" letter to Judge Kenesaw Mountain Landis, January 15, 1942

Babe Ruth

He hit the ball farther than anyone ever had. By late 1919 everyone connected with the baseball world knew who he was. But it wasn't until he moved to New York City that George Herman "Babe" Ruth grabbed the game by the scruff of the neck and shook it silly.

A kid of the streets who learned to play ball while he was an "inmate" at St. Mary's Industrial School for Boys, 19-year-old George made the majors as a pitcher with the Boston Red Sox in 1914. Beginning the next year, he went 78–40 with an ERA under 2.30, helping the club to three World Series titles over four seasons. The left-hander completed a Series-record 29⅔ consec-utive scoreless innings in 1918, yet he was so successful a hitter that manager Ed Barrow began giving him outfield assignments on nonpitching days. The 6′2″ giant liked the arrangement, and when he was allowed to roam the outfield almost exclusively in 1919, he blasted a major-league-record 29 home runs.

Harry Frazee, Red Sox owner, knew he had a prize. Unfortunately, he had something else as well: a lot of debt. He hadn't yet hit his stride as a super impresario. So when the Yankees asked if Ruth were for sale, Frazee sold him to the New York Yankees in January 1920 for a record sum of $125,000—plus a $300,000 loan. Babe put his stamp of approval on the stupidest move in baseball history with a record-shattering 54 homers that year—more homers than 14 of 16 major-league *teams* compiled—and the fun was on. Fans wanted excitement after the hard realities of World War I and the Black Sox scandal, and Ruth supplied it—showing that one swing could accomplish what had previously taken a series of bunts, steals, and slides.

Ruth was the quintessential hero of the Roaring '20s, a ham for the cameras who could back up his bravado. Dominating baseball as no player has before or since, he averaged 47 home runs and 133 RBI during the decade when just four other players hit as many as 40 homers even once. Over his career, Ruth would lead the Yankees to seven pennants and four world championships (belting 15 homers in World Series play), despite regular indulgences in women, booze, and food. He drew screams and suspensions from his managers and screams of delight from kids—to whom he always seemed to appeal and relate best.

Ruth's records are nothing short of remarkable. His 94–46 pitching mark is often overlooked alongside his .690 slugging average and .474 on-base percentage over his career—records never before approached. When the .342 lifetime hitter retired, his 714 home runs were about twice as many as his nearest competitor. That career total and Babe's season high of 60 homers have since been topped, but his impact on the game remains undisputed. He was baseball's most beloved performer—and its finest.

MAJOR LEAGUE TOTALS									
BA	G	AB	R	H	2B	3B	HR	RBI	SB
.342	2,503	8,399	2,174	2,873	506	136	714	2,211	123

"Every big-leaguer and his
wife should teach their
children to pray: 'God bless
Mommy, God bless Daddy,
and *God bless
Babe Ruth.*'"

—YANKEES PITCHER WAITE HOYT,
BASEBALL AS I HAVE KNOWN IT

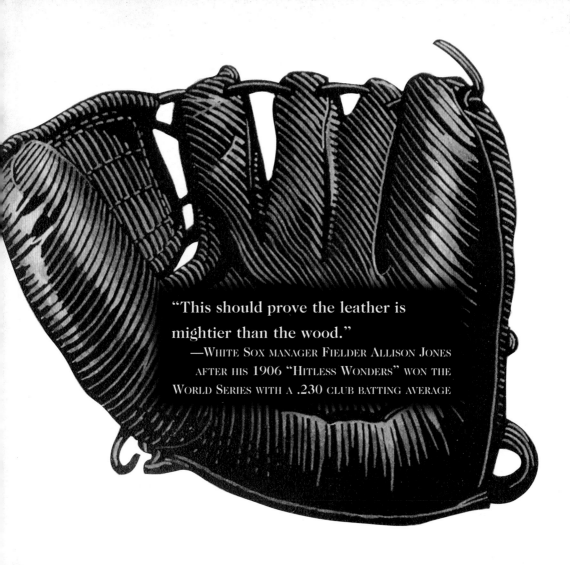

"This should prove the leather is mightier than the wood."
—White Sox manager Fielder Allison Jones after his 1906 "Hitless Wonders" won the World Series with a .230 club batting average

"It could be.... It might be.... *It is! A home run!*"
—*Broadcaster Harry Caray's signature call*

*"It's a great
day for
baseball,"*
Ernie Banks was
fond of saying.
*"Let's play
two!"*
Affectionately
known as Mr. Cub,
Banks belted 512
career home runs—
including 290 at his
beloved Wrigley
Field.

Ted Williams

He struck out in his first major-league at-bat, homered in his last, and during the 21 years between made the art of hitting his personal quest. Ted Williams looked at the goal of wood meeting ball in a scientific way, and if grades were awarded instead of statistics, his achievements—a .344 lifetime average, 521 homers, and a slugging average (.634) second only to Babe Ruth's—would rank him at the head of his class.

The lessons started early: swings taken before, after, and sometimes during school as a pencil-thin teen in San Diego. He and Pacific Coast League teammate Bobby Doerr both signed on with the Red Sox in 1937, and although Williams didn't make the big club the following spring, his parting shot to Boston's starting outfielders who had ridiculed him—"I'll be back and make more money than the three of you combined"— would prove dead-on. A year later he did return, this time for good.

Rookie Williams distinguished himself in 1939 with a .327 average, 31 homers, and an American League–best and rookie-record 145 RBI. In 1941,

Joe DiMaggio captured the attention of the nation with a 56-game hitting streak, but Ted out-hit him .412 to .408 over the course of the streak and finished the season with 37 homers, 120 RBI, and a .406 batting mark—making him the last major-leaguer to reach the charmed .400 level. However, sportswriters awarded the MVP Award to DiMaggio in what turned out to be the first of many times the outspoken Williams (a two-time MVP winner) would be snubbed due to friction with the press.

Williams was a decent left fielder, but when he said he lived for his next at-bat it was no exaggeration. His goal was perfection at the plate; he sought the same from pitchers, and his careful eye enabled him to lead the American League in walks seven times in his first nine full seasons (each time with more than 125). He was criticized for not swinging enough and not hitting in the clutch—this despite an incredible .483 on-base percentage (the best in history) and a .359 lifetime average in September (his best month).

Winner of Triple Crowns in 1942 and '47, Ted led the American League nine times in slugging, six times in batting, six times in runs scored, and four times in homers and RBI. The Player of the Decade for the 1950s hit .388 with 38 homers at age 38 in 1957, won his final batting title (.328) a year later, and slugged 29 long ones in just 310 at-bats in his swan-song season of '60. Despite missing nearly five full seasons as a Navy and Marine flyer and parts of two more to injury, he retired as third on the all-time homer list—and first in many never-ending debates over the greatest hitter of all time.

BA	G	AB	R	H	2B	3B	HR	RBI	SB
.344	2,292	7,706	1,798	2,654	525	71	521	1,839	24

Here's to You, Joe DiMaggio!

After winning AL batting titles in 1939 and '40, Yankees great Joe DiMaggio took hitting to a different level in '41. From May 15 through July 16, Joltin' Joe hit safely in 56 consecutive games (batting .408 over the stretch), shattering Willie Keeler's major-league record of 44. His streak came to an end in Cleveland, due to two great plays by Indians third baseman Ken Keltner. DiMaggio shrugged it off and the next day began another streak, this one continuing for 17 games.

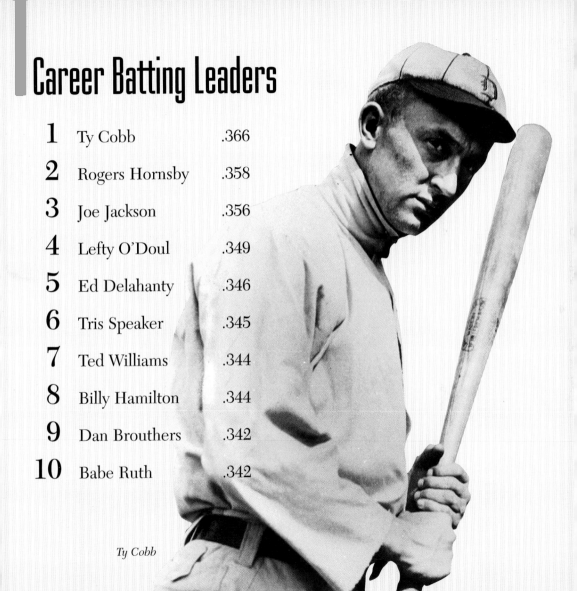

Career Batting Leaders

1	Ty Cobb	.366
2	Rogers Hornsby	.358
3	Joe Jackson	.356
4	Lefty O'Doul	.349
5	Ed Delahanty	.346
6	Tris Speaker	.345
7	Ted Williams	.344
8	Billy Hamilton	.344
9	Dan Brouthers	.342
10	Babe Ruth	.342

Ty Cobb

Sandy Koufax

Over the last five years of his career (1962–1966), Koufax was as dominating as any pitcher ever had been or would be. He decimated National League hitters, going 111–34 and leading the league in ERA each season.

During this five-year run, Sandy won three Cy Young Awards, three pitching "triple crowns," and an MVP Award (1963).

He led Los Angeles to world titles in 1963 (with a 25–5 record, an ERA of 1.88, and 306 strikeouts) and 1965 (26 wins, 2.04 ERA, and 382 Ks). In seven World Series starts lifetime, he went 4–3 with a 0.95 ERA.

Throughout his short career he fired four no-hitters, including a perfect game in 1965.

The youngest player ever inducted into the Hall of Fame, Koufax was forced to retire at age 30 due to the crippling pain of an arthritic elbow.

W	L	ERA	G	CG	IP	H	ER	BB	SO
165	87	2.76	397	137	2,324	1,754	713	817	2,396

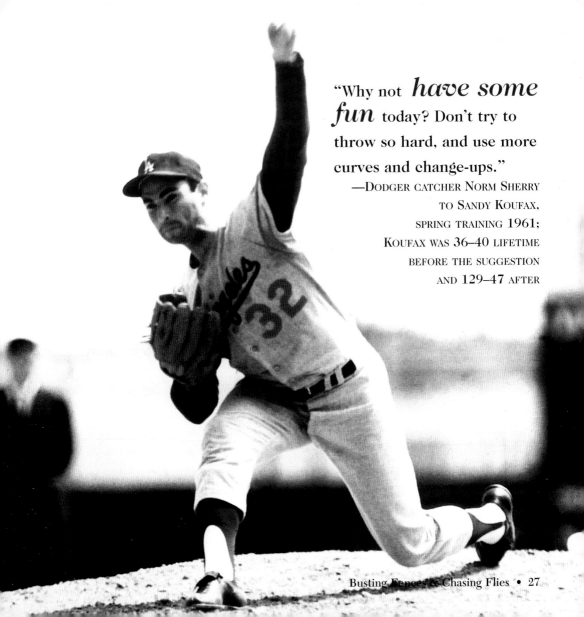

"Why not *have some fun* today? Don't try to throw so hard, and use more curves and change-ups."
—DODGER CATCHER NORM SHERRY TO SANDY KOUFAX, SPRING TRAINING 1961; KOUFAX WAS 36–40 LIFETIME BEFORE THE SUGGESTION AND 129–47 AFTER

Josh Gibson has been credited with almost 800 home runs, many of them blasted unbelievable distances, over the course of his 17-year career in the Negro Leagues. Many think he might have challenged Babe Ruth's single-season home run record, but he never got the chance. He died of a brain hemorrhage in 1947, just three months before Jackie Robinson broke the color line.

"If they came to Josh Gibson today and he were 17 years old, they would have a blank spot on the contract and they'd say, 'Fill the amount in.' *That's how good* Josh Gibson was."

—JUNIOR GILLIAM, *BASEBALL DIGEST, JUNE 1969*

Tony Perez, Johnny Bench, Joe Morgan, and Pete Rose (left to right) *fueled the Big Red Machine, baseball's dominant team of the 1970s. From 1970 to '79, Cincinnati won nearly 60 percent of its games, captured six division titles (plus three second-place finishes), and took a pair of world titles.*

"To **Johnny Bench,** a *Hall of Famer* for sure."

—INSCRIPTION ON BALL SIGNED BY TED WILLIAMS
FOR CINCINNATI'S 20-YEAR-OLD ROOKIE CATCHER,
SPRING TRAINING 1968

The Game's Classiest Players

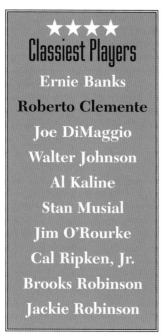

★★★★
Classiest Players
Ernie Banks
Roberto Clemente
Joe DiMaggio
Walter Johnson
Al Kaline
Stan Musial
Jim O'Rourke
Cal Ripken, Jr.
Brooks Robinson
Jackie Robinson

Puerto Rico's Roberto Clemente came to a racially backward town in 1955 and barely spoke the language. The Pittsburgh press ridiculed his poor English and called him a hypochondriac and a malingerer. But fans weren't swayed; they could see his *pride* and *class*. One of the *greatest humanitarians* in the game's history, Clemente lost his life trying to provide aid to Nicaraguan earthquake victims. An elegant statue commemorating him now stands proudly in Pittsburgh.

"I want to be remembered
as a ballplayer who
*gave all he had
to give.*"
—ROBERTO CLEMENTE

Cy Young

At one point, Babe Ruth's 714 career homers was the baseball record most people predicted would never be broken. Once Henry Aaron topped it, Lou Gehrig's streak of 2,130 consecutive games became the popular choice. Since Cal Ripken put that thought to rest, the question arises anew: Five hundred and eleven wins? Twenty-five a year for more than 20 years? Don't worry, Mr. Young, your mark appears safe.

Walter Johnson, Lefty Grove, and others each have been lauded as the greatest pitcher of all time, but Denton True Young's 511 victories remain the benchmark for all hurlers—and far ahead of runner-up Johnson's 417.

Pitching in an era when arms often burned out after a handful of 350-inning seasons, Young exceeded that total 11 times over a 14-year span and was a 20-game winner on a record 15 occasions. His 7,354 innings are more than 1,300 ahead of runner-up Pud Galvin, and even his record 316 losses look secure for the moment.

Growing up just after the Civil War in Gilmore, Ohio, Young picked up his nickname (shortened from "Cyclone") from a minor-league catcher who was impressed by his speed. The hardy, 6′2″ farmhand with the strong legs gained from chasing squirrels reached the majors with the National League Cleveland Spiders in 1890. After a

9–7 debut, he won 20 or more games each of the next nine seasons. Those early years were spent hurling from a pitcher's "box" some 50 feet from home plate. When the distance was increased to 60'6″ with a mound added in 1893, the right-hander didn't seem to miss a beat.

> "Son, I won more games than you'll ever see."
> —CY YOUNG, RESPONDING TO A YOUTHFUL REPORTER

The hard-throwing Young led the NL only twice in wins, and he routinely gave up more hits than innings pitched (although that was the norm in the 1890s). Far from dominating in many of his first 11 seasons, his records grew instead through consistency and durability. His best NL years came in 1892 (36–12 with a league-leading nine shutouts and a 1.93 ERA) and '95 (35–10), but it was after joining the Boston Pilgrims of the new American League in 1901 that Young had his most dominating campaigns. Leading the AL in victories in his first three years with Boston (going 33–10, 32–11, and 28–9), he posted a 1.95 ERA over the span—topping it off in 1903 with two wins as Boston beat Pittsburgh in the first modern World Series.

Author of three no-hitters (including a 1904 perfect game), Young went 21–11 with a 1.26 ERA at age 41. After his career ended in 1911, he lived for 44 more years, attending old-timer's functions and tossing out the first ball at the 1953 World Series. Others may have been flashier, but when the two major leagues honor their best pitchers each season, they do so with a plaque named for the game's winningest hurler—Cy Young.

W	L	ERA	G	CG	IP	H	ER	BB	SO
511	316	2.63	906	750	7,356.0	7,092	2,147	1,217	2,798

Jackie *Breaks* the Color Barrier

After World War II, Brooklyn Dodgers general manager Branch Rickey felt it was time to field the majors' first African-American player—but it had to be someone who was mentally tough. Jackie Robinson was the man. Premiering with the Dodgers on Opening Day 1947, the speedy second baseman endured racist taunts and vicious tags, yet never retaliated. His courage, class, and dynamic play earned him the NL Rookie of the Year Award. In 1997 Robinson's No. 42 was retired by Major League Baseball.

"The way I figured it,
I was even with baseball and

baseball was even with

me. The game had done

much for me, and I had

done much for it."

—Jackie Robinson

1912: Red Sox vs. Giants

The World Series was only just beginning to take hold of the psyche of America in 1912. But this classic clinched the deal forever. Two powerhouse teams, led by ace pitchers Christy Mathewson (New York Giants) and Smokey Joe Wood (Boston Red Sox), banged heads for eight games. It couldn't have been wilder. "There never was another like it," stated *The Spalding Guide.*

The Series was full of clutch plays and intrigue, spectacular pitching and snappy hitting. Wood won the first game 4–3 after fanning the last two batters with runners on second and third. Game 2 ended in a 6–6 tie after 11 innings because of darkness. The final game featured great catches and excruciating bobbles. Boston, capitalizing on Fred Snodgrass's dropped fly ball in the 10th inning, took Game 8.

> "I threw so hard, I thought my arm would fly right off my body."
> —SMOKEY JOE WOOD ON THE NINTH INNING OF GAME 1 OF THE 1912 WORLD SERIES

GAME 1	Boston 4 at New York 3	GAME 5	New York 1 at Boston 2
GAME 2	New York 6 at Boston 6 (11)	GAME 6	Boston 2 at New York 5
GAME 3	New York 2 at Boston 1	GAME 7	New York 11 at Boston 4
GAME 4	Boston 3 at New York 1	GAME 8	New York 2 at Boston 3 (10)

Telling It Like It Is

Red Barber's most able pupil, Vin Scully has created a unique broadcasting style. He always maintains a complete lack of home-team rooting while *weaving words* so poetically descriptive that listeners receive a much greater sense of the game than they do from anyone else. Some of his game calls have been transcribed and anthologized as *classics* in baseball literature. During home games, his voice can be heard on transistor radios throughout Dodger Stadium.

Leo Durocher

I never questioned the integrity of an umpire. Their eyesight, yes.

You don't **save** a pitcher for tomorrow. Tomorrow it might rain.

Show me a **good loser,** and I'll show you *an idiot.*

I believe in rules. I also believe I have a right to test the rules by seeing how far *they can be bent.*

Jimmie Foxx

In his heyday, ol' Double X was called "the right-handed Ruth."
He belted more homers in the 1930s (415) than anyone else,
and when he retired in 1945 his 534 home runs were the second most
in history, trailing only Babe Ruth's 714.

He won his first MVP Award with the Philadelphia A's in 1932
and followed it up with a Triple Crown/MVP year in '33 (.356–48–163).
He took home a third MVP trophy with the Boston Red Sox in '38.

With a .325 lifetime average, 534 homers, 1,922 RBI, and .609 slugging percentage,
Foxx was a first-ballot Hall of Famer.

BA	G	AB	R	H	2B	3B	HR	RBI	SB
.325	2,317	8,134	1,751	2,646	458	125	534	1,922	88

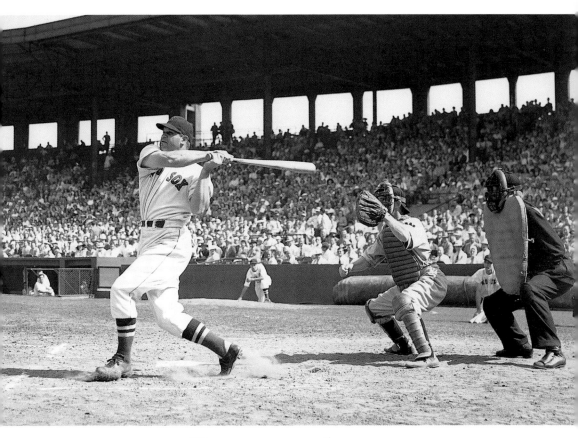

"Next to Joe DiMaggio, *Foxx was the greatest player* I ever saw. When Foxx hit a ball, it sounded like gunfire."

—TED WILLIAMS

The Negro Leagues

Until Jackie Robinson broke the color barrier in 1947, African Americans were banned from Major League Baseball. Some of the best pitchers and sluggers of all time lived out their dreams in the Negro Leagues, which began in 1920 and thrived from 1935 to 1948.

Life in the Negro Leagues was a hardscrabble existence. The players were denied accommodations at many hotels and restaurants, which still catered exclusively to white customers. They stayed at black boarding houses or in the homes of people within the African-American community. In the worst scenario, they would pitch a tent in the outfield and sleep there until the game the next day. Sometimes they would fish for their dinner in nearby lakes and rivers.

But to many of the men who donned Negro League uniforms, the opportunity to play professional baseball was worth enduring such conditions. "It was thrilling to me," said James Moore, who played first base for the Atlanta Black Crackers, Baltimore Elite Giants, and Newark Eagles. "We'd travel from city to city. . . . I was playing baseball and I just loved it."

Negro League teams often played each other in major-league parks. On other occasions, the teams played against American Legion clubs, local police departments, or semipro teams. Players looked forward to exhibition games against major-leaguers, including such stars as Lefty Grove, Jimmie Foxx, and Joe DiMaggio.

"When I first began to play, I thought we were inferior to the white ballplayer," said Moore. "[But] I played against a lot of major-league ballplayers. We beat them some and they beat us some. I realized they were human and we were human. It really made me feel good to be hitting the ball against guys who were in the major leagues."

Pittsburgh Crawfords Oscar Charleston, Rap Dixon, Josh Gibson, Judy Johnson, Jud Wilson (left to right)

Many Negro Leaguers have earned enshrinement in the National Baseball Hall of Fame in Cooperstown. Catcher Josh Gibson, said to be the greatest Negro League hitter of all, belted an estimated 800 home runs in league and exhibition games, including a 580-foot moon shot at Yankee Stadium, and ripped .426 in contests against major-leaguers.

After Robinson debuted with the Brooklyn Dodgers in 1947, other Negro League stars jumped to the majors, from Satchel Paige and Ernie Banks to Willie Mays and Hank Aaron. The last of the Negro Leagues, the Negro American League, disbanded in 1957, thus ending a rich and vibrant era of professional baseball.

Since 1985 the Home Run Derby, played the day before the All-Star Game, has been a fan favorite. Baseball's greatest sluggers try to belt the most soft tosses out of the park before registering 10 "outs" (an out being any hit ball that is not a home run).

MOST HOMERS IN A DERBY	
Bobby Abreu, 2005	41
Miguel Tejada, 2004	27
Albert Pujols, 2003	26
Sammy Sosa, 2000	26

MOST HOMERS IN A ROUND	
Bobby Abreu, 2005	24
David Ortiz, 2005	17
David Wright, 2006	16

LONGEST RECORDED HOMER	
Sammy Sosa, 2002	524 feet

Derby Winners	
2006	Ryan Howard
2005	Bobby Abreu
2004	Miguel Tejada
2003	Garret Anderson
2002	Jason Giambi
2001	Luis Gonzalez
2000	Sammy Sosa
1999	Ken Griffey, Jr.
1998	Ken Griffey, Jr.
1997	Tino Martinez
1996	Barry Bonds
1995	Frank Thomas
1994	Ken Griffey, Jr.
1993	Juan Gonzalez
1992	Mark McGwire
1991	Cal Ripken, Jr.
1990	Ryne Sandberg
1989	Eric Davis, Ruben Sierra
1988	*Canceled due to rain*
1987	Andre Dawson
1986	Darryl Strawberry, Wally Joyner
1985	Dave Parker

Miguel Tejada, 2004

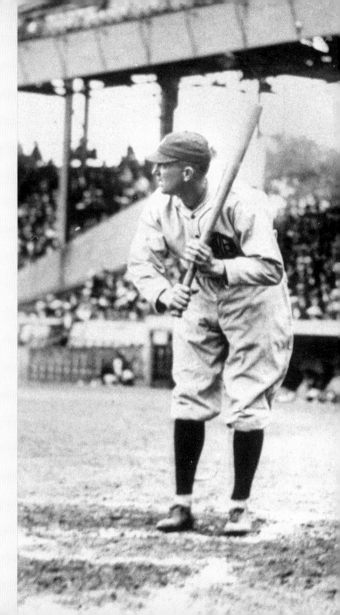

"Every great
batter works on the
theory that the pitcher is
more afraid of him than he
is of the pitcher."

—Ty Cobb,
The Tiger Wore Spikes

Ty Cobb

When a movie on the life of Ty Cobb premiered in theaters in 1994, it was gone in a matter of weeks—most folks showing little interest in paying tribute to the greatest hitter for average (.366) in major-league history. More than 40 years after his death, the reputation of "The Georgia Peach" apparently hasn't changed much. He might have hit and run better than anyone else in baseball, but this was still one nasty son of a gun.

Cobb used his brutal ferocity to attack the game and beat down opponents. Harassed as a scrawny 18-year-old with the Tigers in 1905, he quickly added weight and muscle along with a philosophy of playing hard and trusting no one. He never hit below .316 after his rookie season, and in 1907, at the age of 20, he won his first batting title with a .350 mark. He also led the league with 116 RBI, 212 hits, and 49 stolen bases.

His skills were thereby established; a dead-ball-era hitter who would never accept the home run as a viable part of the game. He would rather bunt than swing for the fences. In the field, he used his great speed and a solid arm to cut down runners, and he registered 20 or more assists on 10 occasions.

But what he did best was hit. His 1907 batting title was the first of nine straight and 12 overall (although two of the batting titles are disputed). Cobb led the Tigers to three straight pennants, from 1907 to '09, and remained the key to Detroit's attack for 20 years. Perennially among American League leaders in slugging and steals (he won six stolen base crowns), he also was the team's most reliable RBI man for many years—averaging 109 a season from 1907 to '12 en route to 1,937 for his career. As a runner, he felt no shame in sliding with his spikes raised high.

Ty won the Triple Crown in 1909 with nine homers, 107 RBI, and a .377 average. Two years later he had perhaps his finest season with a career-high .420 average and league-leading totals in hits (248), doubles (47), triples (24), runs (147), RBI (127), and steals (83). In 1915 he set a stolen base record of 96 that held for nearly 50 years, and in 1922 he hit .400 for the third and last time at the age of 35. He served as player/manager in his final six years with the Tigers, then joined Connie Mack's Athletics in '27 to finish his career. He retired rich from wise investments but virtually devoid of friends. His major-league records for hits (4,189) and steals (892) have since been topped, but his .366 mark will likely endure—along with the sordid reputation of the man who achieved it.

WHO'S WHO in BASEBALL

Price 15c

Facts for Fans

TY COBB

Published by the
BASEBALL MAGAZINE CO.
70 FIFTH AVENUE, NEW YORK

Copyrighted, 1916, by the Baseball Magazine Co., New York

BA	G	AB	R	H	2B	3B	HR	RBI	SB
.366	3,034	11,429	2,245	4,189	724	297	117	1,937	892

Oriole Park at Camden Yards, Baltimore

Completed in 1992, Camden Yards was the first of the magnificent retro-ballparks. Part of the urban landscape, the park is buffered by the hundred-year-old B&O Warehouse beyond the right-field fence. Inside, Camden Yards boasts comfortable seats, a dual-level bullpen, an ivy-covered wall, and even fresh flowers along the walkways. Some fans come just for the beverages and food, which includes freshly squeezed lemonade and Boog Powell's succulent barbecue.

Rogers Hornsby

From 1921 to 1925, through 696 games, 2,679 at-bats, and countless doubleheaders in the sweltering St. Louis sun, Hornsby *averaged* a .402 batting mark—perhaps the greatest hitting stretch ever.

His lifetime .358 batting average is the NL record and is second only to Ty Cobb in major-league history.

Hornsby eclipsed the much-vaunted .400 mark three times, including a 20th-century-record .424 for the St. Louis Cardinals in 1924.

The man known as "Rajah" won six consecutive batting titles from 1920 to '25 and captured the National League Triple Crown in 1922 (.401–42–152) and 1925 (.403–39–143).

BA	G	AB	R	H	2B	3B	HR	RBI	SB
.358	2,259	8,173	1,579	2,930	541	169	301	1,584	135

"Any ballplayer that don't sign autographs for little kids ain't an American."

—ROGERS HORNSBY

Hack Wilson,
*at 5'6" and a rock-solid 190
pounds, was power personified.
In 1930 he was absolutely
unstoppable: 56 homers,
191 RBI, and 423 total bases.*

"I'd *walk* me."
—WILLIE McCOVEY ON HOW HE
WOULD PITCH TO HIMSELF,
BASEBALL DIGEST,
SEPTEMBER 1971

CHAPTER TWO

Cracks of the Bat, *Plays* at the Plate & *Fun* in the Field

"Whoever wants to know *the heart and mind* of America had better learn baseball, the rules and realities of the game."

—JACQUES BARZUN, PHILOSOPHY PROFESSOR

With a record 17 straight 15-win seasons, Greg Maddux may be the most consistent pitcher in baseball history. A cerebral control artist who exploits hitters' weaknesses, Maddux went 19–2 with a 1.63 ERA for Atlanta in 1995 and won his 300th game with the Cubs in 2004. He also took home his 15th Gold Glove Award in '05 and is a 4-time Cy Young Award winner (1992–1995).

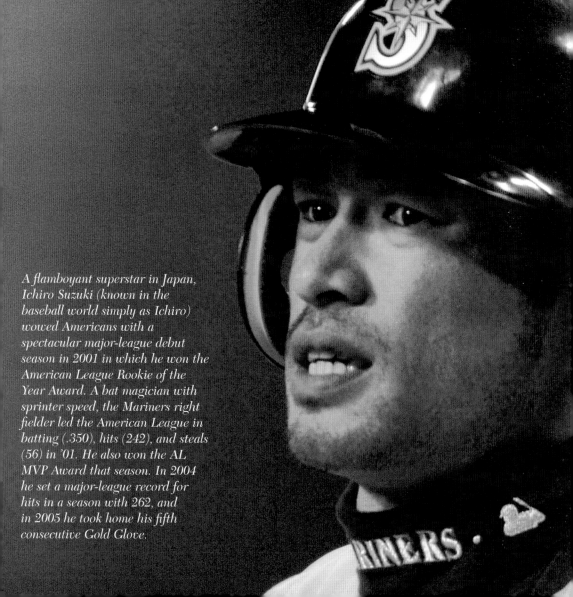

A flamboyant superstar in Japan, Ichiro Suzuki (known in the baseball world simply as Ichiro) wowed Americans with a spectacular major-league debut season in 2001 in which he won the American League Rookie of the Year Award. A bat magician with sprinter speed, the Mariners right fielder led the American League in batting (.350), hits (242), and steals (56) in '01. He also won the AL MVP Award that season. In 2004 he set a major-league record for hits in a season with 262, and in 2005 he took home his fifth consecutive Gold Glove.

Presidential Pitchin'

One of baseball's best-preserved traditions is that of the president throwing out the first ball of the season. It is a gesture that has come to symbolize everything patriotic about the game and has endured despite the departure of the Washington Senators for Texas in 1971.

> "I am glad to hear of their coming, but they will have to wait a few minutes till I get my turn at bat."
> —ABRAHAM LINCOLN, ON BEING INFORMED OF HIS NOMINATION FOR PRESIDENT, 1860

Fittingly, the first chief executive to perform the ritual was one of the most ardent fans ever to occupy the White House—William Howard Taft. Legend has it that Taft, a chunky power hitter as a lad, was offered a big-league contract by Cincinnati before he threw out his arm. Nevertheless, the arm was healthy enough on April 14, 1910, when the 300-pounder was on hand at Washington's National Park to take in the opener between the Senators and Athletics at the invitation of American League President Ban Johnson. Taft, the top-hatted tosser, removed his kid gloves and let loose with a low peg to Senators starter Walter Johnson, and a tradition was born. Taft was back at National Park to christen the 1911 season, and every president since except Jimmy Carter has performed the feat at least once during office—although for years they had to travel to Baltimore to do so. With the arrival of the Nationals in D.C. in 2005, the president will no longer have to travel.

"A couple of years ago, they told me I was **too young** to be President and you were **too old** to be playing baseball. But we fooled them."
—45-YEAR-OLD JOHN F. KENNEDY TO 41-YEAR-OLD STAN MUSIAL AT THE 1962 ALL-STAR GAME

For manager Tommy Lasorda, a good day meant a plate of linguini, hugs all around, and another victory for his beloved L.A. Dodgers. In 21 years of *"bleeding Dodger blue,"* Hall of Famer Lasorda won two world titles and finished first or second in the NL West 13 times.

"When **Steve and I** die, we're going to be buried *60 feet, six inches* apart."

—Tim McCarver *(LEFT)*, "PERSONAL" CATCHER FOR STEVE CARLTON *(RIGHT)* MUCH OF HIS CAREER, *THE PITCHER*

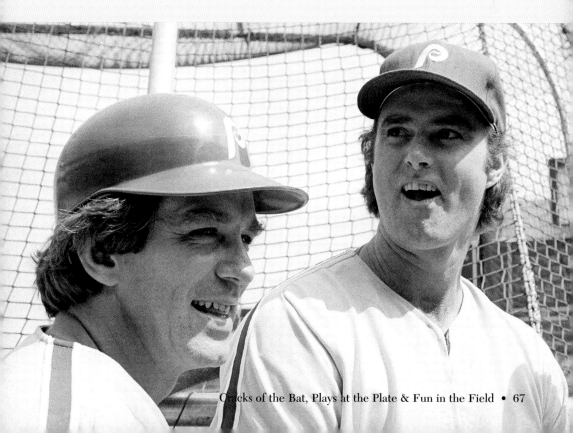

Luis Aparicio

set a standard of athleticism for shortstops with his acrobatic defense and baseline-burning speed. "Little Louie" won nine Gold Gloves and the same number of consecutive stolen-base titles.

Lou Brock was among the first players to truly change games—and the game itself—with his speed. Traded by the Cubs to St. Louis in 1964, he stole 43 bases that year to spark the Cardinals to the World Series.

Yogi Berra

Seldom has a person's exterior allowed for more misconceptions about his character or capabilities than in the case of Lawrence Peter Berra. A squat, funny-looking kid from a St. Louis neighborhood known as "Dago Hill," Berra developed a reputation for being uncouth and unworldly and saying things that made no sense. In reality this man, whose appearance and disposition earned him the nickname "Yogi," was a shrewd and successful businessman, one of the most popular Americans of the 20th century, and the most consistently superb catcher of baseball's Golden Era.

The final statement is no stretch. Roy Campanella, Johnny Bench, and others had periods in which their accomplishments outshone Berra's best seasons, but for year-in and year-out excellence, Yogi stands alone. In 14 full seasons from 1948 to '61, the 5'8" receiver with the infectious grin averaged 23 homers and 94 RBI, led American League catchers in games caught and total chances eight times each, and from 1957 to '59 went a stretch of 148 games and 950 chances without an error. Not coincidentally, he played on 14 pennant-winners and 10 world-championship clubs in his 19-year career, setting records for World Series games, hits, and doubles along the way.

Berra reached the Yankees late in 1946 after a stint in the Navy. Over the next two years, he split time as a backup catcher and outfielder. As the Yankees' starting catcher in 1948, Yogi rapped .305 with 14 homers and 98 RBI. Thus began a career of sustained brilliance. Starting in 1949, Berra amassed at least 20 home runs and 82 RBI for 10 straight years, reaching heights of 30 homers twice (then an American League record for catchers), 125 RBI (during a string of four straight 100-RBI seasons), and a top batting average of .322 in 1950. A great guess hitter who performed best in the clutch, Berra was named MVP in 1951, '54, and '55, yet was so consistent that his award-winning years were indistinguishable from the rest.

Defensive tutoring from Hall of Famer Bill Dickey made Yogi a sure-handed receiver. His expert handling of

> "He seemed to be doing everything wrong, yet everything came out right. He stopped everything behind the plate and hit everything in front of it."—MEL OTT

pitchers, achieved by focusing on their varying personalities, was part of his own brand of genius.

Berra may have been known for spouting malapropisms and making people scratch their heads and chuckle, but the Hall of Famer usually got his point across—along with a laugh. Yogi was probably the most popular ballplayer of his generation, and his personality translated well to managing. He was just the second manager—after Joe McCarthy—to win pennants in both leagues, doing it with both the Yankees (1964) and Mets ('73). Some may still think him a jokester; in reality, he is a true American success story.

MAJOR LEAGUE TOTALS									
BA	G	AB	R	H	2B	3B	HR	RBI	SB
.285	2,120	7,555	1,175	2,150	321	49	358	1,430	30

Roger Clemens

Still overpowering hitters in his 40s, Clemens ranks second
on the all-time list in career strikeouts and
is eighth in total victories.

"The Rocket" has won more Cy Young Awards (seven) than
any other big-league pitcher.

On September 18, 1996, Clemens tied his own record of striking out 20 in a
9-inning game, which he first accomplished on April 29, 1986.

Answering critics who said he was washed up, Clemens won the AL
"pitcher triple crown" with Toronto in 1997 (21–7, 2.05 ERA, and 292 Ks) and
repeated the feat in 1998 (20–6, 2.65, 271).

In 1998–99, Clemens set an American League record by posting
20 consecutive victories.

W	L	ERA	G	CG	IP	H	ER	BB	SO
348	178	3.10	691	118	4,818	4,086	1,833	1,549	4,604

Clemens stormed to the
American League
MVP Award in 1986
with Boston.

Baseball's Best Bunters

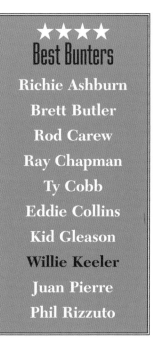

★★★★
Best Bunters

Richie Ashburn
Brett Butler
Rod Carew
Ray Chapman
Ty Cobb
Eddie Collins
Kid Gleason
Willie Keeler
Juan Pierre
Phil Rizzuto

Wee Willie Keeler, a turn-of-the-century star, was one of the game's greatest *"scientific" hitters*, using his smarts to wring every hit he could out of the dead ball. Keeler was a founding father of the *"Baltimore chop,"* swatting the ball directly downward on the hard Oriole infield in order to beat it out for a hit. Quite simply, his bunting was a precision act. The 5′4″ Keeler shared his wisdom by advising hitters simply to *"hit 'em where they ain't."*

The Catch

The Cleveland Indians won an American League–record 111 games in 1954, but they hadn't faced the likes of the New York Giants' Willie Mays. In Game 1 of the World Series, Cleveland's Vic Wertz blasted one to the deep recesses of the Polo Grounds' center field. Running full speed toward the wall, Mays made an over-the-shoulder catch—then, in perhaps the most amazing part of the play, fired a howitzer to the infield to prevent the go-ahead run from scoring. "The Catch" sparked New York to victory and a stunning four-game sweep.

A national phenomenon in 1976, Detroit rookie Mark "The Bird" Fidrych talked to the ball, hand-groomed the pitcher's mound, and sprinted back to the dugout after the third out. He also went 19–9 and led the league in ERA (2.34) and complete games (24), earning the AL Rookie of the Year Award.

"When I get **through managing,** I'm going to
open up a kindergarten."

—YANKEES MANAGER BILLY MARTIN

Notable Nicknames

Luke "Old Aches and Pains" Appling

Steve "Bye-Bye" Balboni

Pee Wee Butts

Will "The Thrill" Clark

Fidgety Phil Collins

Pickles Dillhoefer

Spittin' Bill Doak

Leo "The Lip" Durocher

Al "The Mad Hungarian" Hrabosky

Tony "Poosh 'Em Up" Lazzeri

Aurelio "Señor Smoke" Lopez

Sal "The Barber" Maglie

Raw Meat Bill Rodgers

Harry "Suitcase" Simpson

Dick "Dr. Strangeglove" Stuart

1931: Cardinals vs. Athletics

They weren't called the "Gashouse Gang" just yet, but this St. Louis Cardinals team was definitely smoking against the proud and potent Philadelphia Athletics of Connie Mack. This Mack club could have been the finest ever. The A's were making their third consecutive World Series appearance, averaging more than 104 wins each year. Five of their members are now enshrined in the Hall of Fame.

But the pesky Cards didn't care, even though the same A's had whipped them in six games in the '30 Series. The key was the amazing performance of Pepper Martin *(right)* for St. Louis. He undressed the mighty A's with his boisterous batting (12-for-24) and dazzling baserunning (five steals). And with the winning run at the plate for the A's in the ninth inning of Game 7, the man who grabbed the fly ball to end it all was ... Pepper Martin.

GAME 1	Philadelphia 6 at St. Louis 2	GAME 5	St. Louis 5 at Philadelphia 1
GAME 2	Philadelphia 0 at St. Louis 2	GAME 6	Philadelphia 8 at St. Louis 1
GAME 3	St. Louis 5 at Philadelphia 2	GAME 7	Philadelphia 2 at St. Louis 4
GAME 4	St. Louis 0 at Philadelphia 3		

Career Hit Leaders

1   Pete Rose   4,256

2   Ty Cobb   4,189

3   Hank Aaron   3,771

4   Stan Musial   3,630

5   Tris Speaker   3,514

6   Carl Yastrzemski   3,419

7   Cap Anson   3,418

8   Honus Wagner   3,415

9   Paul Molitor   3,319

10   Eddie Collins   3,315

Pete Rose

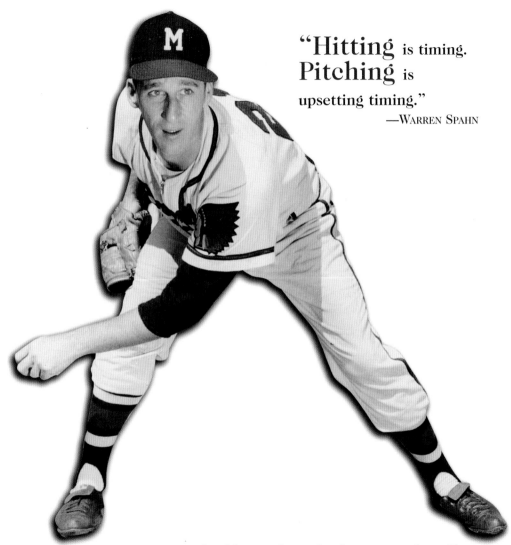

"**Hitting** is timing.
Pitching is
upsetting timing."

—WARREN SPAHN

"I would be the *laughingstock of the league* if I took the best left-handed pitcher in the league and put him in the outfield."

—RED SOX MANAGER ED BARROW IN 1918
ON MOVING BABE RUTH FROM THE MOUND TO A FULL-TIME POSITION,
THE SPORTING NEWS

"Ruth made a *grave mistake* when he gave up pitching. Working once a week, he might have lasted a long time and become a *great star.*"

—TRIS SPEAKER ON BABE RUTH'S SWITCH
TO THE OUTFIELD, 1919

"I believe *the sale of Babe Ruth* will ultimately strengthen the team."

—RED SOX OWNER HARRY FRAZEE, WHO IN JANUARY 1920
SOLD THE GREATEST PLAYER IN BASEBALL HISTORY
TO THE YANKEES

"Sixty. Count 'em. Sixty! Let's see some other SOB match that!"

—BABE RUTH IN THE YANKEE LOCKER ROOM AFTER HITTING HIS 60TH HOMER OF THE SEASON, SEPTEMBER 30, 1927, *CLOUT! THE TOP HOME RUNS IN BASEBALL HISTORY*

Ebbets Field, Brooklyn

From 1913 to 1957, Ebbets Field, intimate and unique, hosted the Brooklyn Dodgers and their outrageous fans. The "Dodger Sym-Phony," who loved to play "Three Blind Mice" when the umpires appeared, called this stadium home. The outfield fences jutted every which way, while the upper deck hung out over the field. Batters hoped to hit clothier Abe Stark's ad in right field, which stated: "Hit Sign, Win Suit." Today's retro-ballparks pay homage to this classic park.

Champion of the Little Guy

He brought exploding scoreboards, a 42-year-old rookie, and a 3'7" pinch hitter to the major leagues, and while he didn't mix too well with his fellow owners, he certainly gave the fans a good time. Through a wild life spent putting forth gim-

micks, stunts, and some very good teams, Bill Veeck offered others the chance to enjoy the game as much as he did while living up to his Hall of Fame epitaph: "Champion of the Little Guy."

Veeck's impact on baseball began early. As a teenager working for the Chicago Cubs club owned by his father, he planted the seeds from which burst forth the ivy that still covers the out-field walls of Wrigley Field. He quit college at age 19 to become full-time treasurer of the Cubs, then was off to minor-league Milwaukee—where, with the help of home-plate weddings, fireworks, and pig give-aways, he turned a mori-bund franchise into a club so popular it prompted Boston Braves owner Lou Perini to move his big-league team to Wisconsin a decade later. Veeck had a wooden leg courtesy of World War II, but most folks still found it impossible to keep up with "The Maverick" and his shenanigans.

It was more of the same in the majors. Veeck built a World Series champion in Cleveland by 1948. And by dreaming up promotions such as "Good Ol' Joe Early" night—when he showered an average fan with gifts—he demolished Yankee attendance records by drawing more than 2.6 million fans.

One of his wildest moves in '48 was bringing aboard ancient "rookie" pitcher and Negro League legend Satchel Paige, who went 6–1. A year earlier, when Veeck broke the American League color line by bringing Larry Doby to Cleveland, he received 20,000 letters from incensed fans and answered each by hand. After the Indians were officially eliminated from the 1949 pennant race, the Maverick led a funeral cortege onto the field and buried the club's '48 championship banner.

A few years later Veeck sold the Tribe and purchased the dismal St. Louis Browns, more than doubling attendance for a seventh-place club thanks to stunts like the 1951 appearance of No. ⅛ Eddie Gaedel—whose 3'7" frame prompted a walk on four pitches. From there it was on to the White Sox, where Veeck copped another pennant in 1959 and set club attendance marks due in part to a scoreboard that shot off fireworks following home runs. The old guard of ownership never appreciated his free spirit, but he always had the love of his players and, most important, the fans. Late in life he often sat in the Wrigley Field bleachers, shirtless and with his wooden leg serving as a beer coaster and ashtray.

Satchel Paige with Bill Veeck

Speaker holds the major-league record for career doubles with 792, including a whopping 59 in 1923.

He ranks among the top six in ML history in career batting, hits, and triples, and he batted in the .380s five times throughout his stellar career, including .383 in his AL MVP season of 1912. Speaker remains the only major-leaguer to rack up three hitting streaks of 20 games or longer in the same season.

Considered the greatest defensive outfielder of his day, "The Gray Eagle" (called that due to his prematurely graying hair) is the majors' all-time leader in outfield assists (448).

BA	G	AB	R	H	2B	3B	HR	RBI	SB
.344	2,789	10,208	1,881	3,515	792	223	117	1,559	433

His name has
not maintained
quite the same
luster of Babe
Ruth and Ty
Cobb, but for
many years
Tris
Speaker
was usually
the third man
mentioned as
one of the
greatest
outfielders
of all time.

The Shot Heard 'Round the World

After trailing crosstown rival Brooklyn by 13½ games on August 11, 1951, the New York Giants stunningly caught the Dodgers, forcing a three-game playoff. Down 4–2 in the bottom of the ninth in Game 3, New York sent Bobby Thomson to the plate with two men on—and he promptly drilled one over the left-field fence. "The Giants win the pennant!" blared broadcaster Russ Hodges. "And they're going crazy!" Thomson's homer was soon dubbed the "shot heard 'round the world."

"Branca throws...There's a long drive! It's going to be...I do believe! The Giants win the pennant! *The Giants win the pennant!* The Giants win the pennant!"

—Radio broadcaster Russ Hodges, October 3, 1951

"Hey, Mac, didn't that one
sound a bit low?"
—Lefty Gomez to the umpire after
taking a called strike three from Bob
Feller, *Young Baseball Champions*

Bob Feller

At just 15 years and 10 months old, Joe Nuxhall became the youngest man ever to play in a major-league game when he worked two-thirds of an inning for the Cincinnati Reds on June 10, 1944.

The Cardinals' Enos Slaughter was playing with a broken elbow when he made his "mad dash"—a sprint from first base to home on Harry Walker's hit that decided the 1946 World Series.

Career Stolen Base Leaders

1	Rickey Henderson	1,406
2	Lou Brock	938
3	Billy Hamilton	912
4	Ty Cobb	892
5	Tim Raines	808
6	Vince Coleman	752
7	Eddie Collins	744
8	Arlie Latham	739
9	Max Carey	738
10	Honus Wagner	722

Rickey Henderson

1924: Senators vs. Giants

This was the season legendary Washington Senators hurler Walter Johnson was supposed to triumph after spending years without winning a pennant. But he lost his first two starts to the New York Giants, and Washington, under rookie manager Bucky Harris, was fighting to hold on. Three of the first six games were decided by one run—one in extra innings.

The seventh game was beyond belief. Giants catcher Hank Gowdy got his foot stuck in his face mask, and two hits bounced over Giants third baseman Fred Lindstrom's head—including the game-winning hit in the 12th inning. The winning pitcher? Walter Johnson. Afterward, commissioner Kenesaw Mountain Landis watched the celebrating Washington fans and said, "Are we seeing the high point of this thing we love? Are we looking at the crest of the institution we know as professional American baseball?"

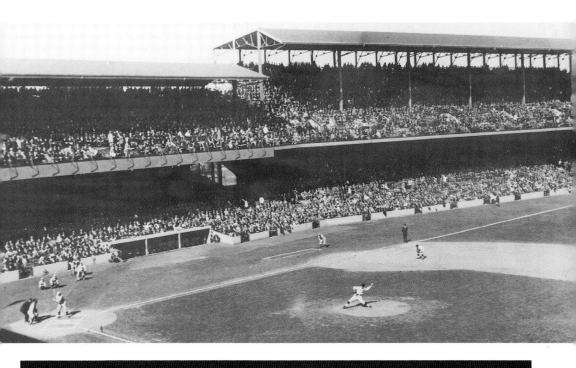

George Brett was one of the most consistent hitters of his era. A career-long Royal, he ripped .390 in 1980 and won batting titles in the 1970s, '80s, and '90s. He is the only big-leaguer with 3,000 hits, 300 homers, 600 doubles, 100 triples, and 200 steals.

"... sometimes in this game it's *as good to be lucky* as it is to *be good.*"

—VIDA BLUE, *VIDA: HIS OWN STORY*

The big-league career of one-armed Pete Gray, called up in 1945 to help fill St. Louis's roster during WWII, lasted only 77 games, over which he batted .218.

"[Cap] Anson, who was our manager, was so good, in fact, that he was arrogant about it. He'd always take two strikes just to defy the pitchers, then get his hit."

—CLARK GRIFFITH,
BASEBALL DIGEST, MARCH 1943

The Daffy Dizzy Dean

"If you say you're going to do it, and you go out and do it, it ain't bragging." Jay Hanna Dean lived by this credo throughout his colorful National League pitching career, and he usually proved it right. He may have lived up to his nickname of "Dizzy" with the humorous way he mangled the English language and cavorted on and off the field, but this was one country boy who could back up his actions with heroics matched by few performers before or since.

Dubbed "Dizzy" by an Army sergeant for his quirky way of viewing the world, the right-hander was already making headlines for showing up late, trash-talking veterans, and striking out batters in bunches by the time he reached his first spring training with the Cardinals in 1931. Within two years, at the ripe age of 22, he was a 20-game winner and owned the major-league strikeout record with 17 whiffs in one game.

Dean really hit his prime in 1934, the year brother Paul ("Daffy") joined him in the Cardinals rotation. "Me 'n Paul will win 45 games," Diz boasted, and while some scoffed, the duo was more than up to the task. Paul went 19–11, his "veteran" brother 30–7 despite twice holding sit-down strikes— once to get Paul a raise on his $3,000 salary. In September, the Deans started both ends of a doubleheader against Brooklyn. Dizzy held the Dodgers hitless until the eighth inning before settling for a three-hitter, but when Paul threw a no-hitter in the nightcap, Diz told writers, "Gee, if I'd known Paul was gonna do it, I'd done it too."

The Deans each won two games in the World Series for the victorious Cards that fall, but Dizzy's days at the top were numbered. A line drive off the bat of Cleveland's Earl Averill in the '37 All-Star Game broke Dean's big toe, and by coming back too soon and altering his motion he developed a sore arm. He hung on gamely for a few more years, then turned to a highly successful broadcasting career—where he described how runners "slud into third," mediocre pitchers had "nothin' on the ball 'cept a cover," and weak batters "couldn't get a hit with a hoe." After repeatedly poking fun at the hapless 1947 Browns on radio, he was dared by club president Bill DeWitt to do better. Coming out of a six-year retirement for one day to throw four shutout innings, he proved himself right a final time.

Daffy (left) *and Dizzy Dean*

CHAPTER THREE

Rounding the Bases

"You spend a good piece of your life *gripping a baseball* and in the end it turns out that it was the other way around all the time."

—JIM BOUTON, *BALL FOUR*

Honoring Greatness

In 1936, baseball came up with the ultimate reward for its stars: a Hall of Fame. The Depression-weary baseball establishment, desperate for a gimmick that might start the turnstiles spinning again, began making plans for the game's 100th birthday. Those plans would link the Centennial with a National Baseball Hall of Fame and Museum in Cooperstown, New York.

Two elections were held in 1936 to determine who should be enshrined in the newly created Baseball Hall of Fame: one by the 226 members of the Baseball Writers Association of America; the other by a special 78-member veterans committee. Interestingly, no criteria were ever spelled out for what made someone a Hall of Famer. Stats? Character? Winning? A combination? It just seemed obvious; anyone could tell who was a Hall of Famer and who wasn't.

The only five able to muster the required 75 percent of either committee's vote were all retired players. No fan could argue with the choices: Ty Cobb (222 votes), Babe Ruth and Honus Wagner (215 each), Christy Mathewson (205), and Walter Johnson (189). In the next three years, 21 more men were chosen in additional elections, from Nap Lajoie and Pete Alexander to Wee Willie Keeler and George Sisler.

Today, the bronze plaques that hang in the Hall of Fame gallery immortalize more than 250 of baseball's greatest stars.

Ten of the eleven living Hall of Fame inductees in 1939: (back row, from left) Honus Wagner, Grover Cleveland Alexander, Tris Speaker, Nap Lajoie, George Sisler, Walter Johnson; (front row, from left) Eddie Collins, Babe Ruth, Connie Mack, Cy Young.

Rose *Breaks the Ty*

After chasing Ty Cobb's career hit record (4,191) for years,

Cincinnati's Pete Rose broke the hallowed mark at home on

September 11, 1985. Riverfront

Stadium erupted when he lined a

single to left-center off San Diego's

Eric Show. While hugging first base

coach Tommy Helms, the new hit

king broke into tears. Afterward,

Rose said he would have maintained

his composure if the fans hadn't

cheered for so long.

She Fanned the Babe

Though Babe Ruth and Lou Gehrig were two of baseball's greatest hitters, a woman once struck them out. It happened in 1931, when the Yankees stopped in Chattanooga en route home from spring training camp. Joe

Jackie Mitchell, Babe Ruth, and Lou Gehrig

Engel, owner of the independent team there, had a widespread reputation for innovative ideas, but this one was the topper. He unveiled a local pitching phenomenon named Jackie Mitchell, who proceeded to strike out Ruth and fellow slugger Lou Gehrig—a feat that made national headlines.

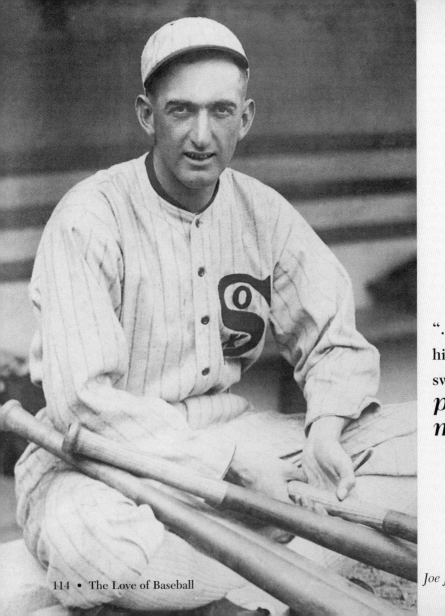

"... the perfect hitter. **Joe's** swing was *purely magical.*"

—TY COBB ON JOE JACKSON, *BASEBALL DIGEST,* JULY 1973

Joe Jackson

Shoeless Joe Jackson may or may not have taken part in the conspiracy by White Sox players to throw the 1919 World Series—he hit .375 and fielded flawlessly over the eight-game classic. But his banishment from the majors along with seven teammates more than a year later ensured that his record would be forever tainted. Even though his name *does not adorn* a Hall of Fame plaque, he certainly has the qualifications—most notably a .356 career average (third all-time) and a .517 slugging mark.

Jackie Robinson

Statistics don't always do great players justice, but in Jackie Robinson's case numbers are almost irrelevant. Sure, Robinson was a lifetime .311 hitter who spearheaded six pennants and a world championship for the Brooklyn Dodgers, but it was as a crusader for his and

all people that Jackie stood out. Long after his statistics are forgotten, he will continue to stand as one of the most significant figures in American history.

Born in a shack on a Georgia cotton field, this grandson of a slave and son of sharecroppers was UCLA's first four-sport star before he enlisted in the Army during World War II. After his discharge, Robinson joined the Kansas City Monarchs of the Negro Leagues as debate over the major-league color ban

increased. One of three players given a sham tryout by the Boston Red Sox in April 1945, Jackie received a far more sincere gesture from Dodgers general manager Branch Rickey a few months later—a contract making him the first black player signed by a major-league organization in more than half a century. Why Robinson? Because Rickey saw in Jackie the blend of intelligence, character, and iron will needed to endure the challenges ahead.

After leading the International League in batting (.349) for minor-league Montreal in '46, Jackie made the Dodgers the following spring. As a rookie, he was taunted, spiked on the bases, and thrown at by racist pitchers. But true to his word to Mr. Rickey,

Robinson stayed calm and let his play do the talking.

It spoke loud and clear, as Robinson electrified crowds with his running (a league-high 29 steals) and production (.297 with 12 homers and 125 runs scored). The Dodgers won the pennant and set an NL attendance record, and Jackie was voted the first National League Rookie of the Year. Teammates who once considered passing a petition against his playing now defended him in on-field incidents, and Robinson grew into a leadership role on one of the finest clubs in Brooklyn history.

Jackie became an outstanding defensive second baseman who led the NL in double plays four straight years, and he had 19 career steals of home—once stealing his way around the bases to get there. In 1949 he won the NL MVP Award, leading the league in batting (.342) and steals (37) while scoring 122 runs and driving in 124. He averaged .329 with 108 runs and 93 RBI from 1949 to '53 before retiring three years later.

Robinson spoke out against injustice until diabetes cut him down in 1972 at age 53. In his autobiography, published just after his death, Robinson stated that as a black American he "never had it made," but what he endured and what he achieved made it easier for those who followed.

> "Those who tangled with him always admitted afterward that he was a man's man, a person who would not compromise his convictions."
> —BASEBALL WRITER WENDELL SMITH ON ROBINSON, *BASEBALL DIGEST,* JANUARY 1973

BA	G	AB	R	H	2B	3B	HR	RBI	SB
.311	1,382	4,877	947	1,518	273	54	137	734	197

The Greatest Teams Ever

Best Teams

1902 Pirates
1904–05 Giants
1906–08 Cubs
1927 Yankees
1929–31 Athletics
1936–39 Yankees
1949–53 Yankees
1954 Indians
1975–76 Reds
1996–2001 Yankees

The 1927 New York Yankees led the American League in home runs, belting 102 more than the No. 2 team on the list. Their *"Murderer's Row"* lineup featured Babe Ruth (.356–60–164), Lou Gehrig (.373–47–175), Bob Meusel (.337–8–103), and Earle Combs (.356–6–64). New York went 110–44 and easily swept Pittsburgh in the World Series.

"The power of the team *blinded* onlookers to the skill and smoothness of its fielding. Enemy teams *cracked* and *broke* wide open before their assaults."

—FRANK GRAHAM ON THE 1927 YANKEES, *THE NEW YORK YANKEES*

Babe Ruth (left) *and Lou Gehrig* (right)

With an arm that only the foolish challenged, catcher Ivan Rodriguez has won 11 Gold Gloves and the 1999 AL MVP Award. He led the Marlins to the 2003 world title and helped the Tigers reach the 2006 playoffs.

OFFICIAL ALL-STAR
SPORT PARADE
SPRING-SUMMER 1964

OFFICIAL ALL-STAR
BY THE EDITORS OF OFFICIAL SPORTS, INC.

50¢

SPORT PARADE

WILLIE MAYS

84 PAGES ON
60 OF THE
GREATEST
STARS IN
SPORTS

Mickey Mantle
Willie Mays
Sandy Koufax
Hank Aaron
plus
30 OTHER TOP
DIAMOND
PERSONALITIES

PRO-FOOTBALL SECTION

Y. A. Tittle
Jimmy Brown
17 Great Gridders In All

SPECIAL BONUS SECTION
THE RECORD-BREAKERS
track · field · swimming
John Pennel · Bob Hayes · Gar Gubner and 6 others

"**We** Who Are About to
Cry *Salute You.*"

—SIGN HANGING FROM THE
LEFT-FIELD STANDS AT SHEA
STADIUM ON THE NIGHT
WILLIE MAYS SAID GOOD-BYE
TO BASEBALL AND HIS FANS,
SEPTEMBER 1973

Johnny Bench

Named the starting catcher on major-league baseball's All-Century Team,
Bench had it all: size, strength, quickness, and a terrifying arm.

He invented the art of one-handed catching, the perfect style to gun down
the newer and faster basestealers of his era.

The much-honored catcher was named Rookie of the Year in 1968,
was elected to 14 All-Star Teams, took home 10 consecutive
Gold Glove Awards (1968–1977), and earned NL MVP honors in 1970 and '72.

Bench, who led the Reds to four World Series and two world titles (1975 and '76),
set the major-league record for career home runs by a catcher
during his 17 seasons with Cincinnati.

BA	G	AB	R	H	2B	3B	HR	RBI	SB
.267	2,158	7,658	1,091	2,048	381	24	389	1,376	68

"I don't want to *embarrass any other catcher* by comparing them to Johnny Bench."

—Sparky Anderson

Three Players, One Card

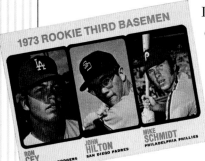

1973 ROOKIE THIRD BASEMEN

RON CEY
LOS ANGELES DODGERS

JOHN HILTON
SAN DIEGO PADRES

MIKE SCHMIDT
PHILADELPHIA PHILLIES

In today's competitive market, baseball-card manufacturers produce everything from gold-tipped cards to holographic images of stars in action.

A generation ago, however, only one card company really mattered: Topps. Every kid was out to get the same players and the same rock-hard gum as each new series was released throughout the summer. Not nearly as glamorous or flashy as today's cards, those of decades past seemed to have more character even if their short-comings were more evident.

If a player was traded too late for a picture to be taken of him in his new uniform, there was no computerized method for fixing things; a new cap and jersey simply were painted over the old photo. Rookies didn't earn their own cards before ever playing a game, as even high school draft picks do today; instead they shared space with one, two, or even three other hopefuls. Collectors were left to wonder which third baseman would make it—Ron Cey, John Hilton, or Mike Schmidt.

Even the players themselves seemed to have more fun with cards then, sometimes batting or pitching from the wrong direction while posing for photographers. In 1969 Aurelio Rodriguez of the Angels pulled perhaps the biggest prank of all when he had a batboy pose for his card photo. Topps didn't realize it had been duped until it was too late—much to collectors' delight.

Retained as Cleveland's player/manager in 1948 only because the
fans voted 10-to-1 to do so, Lou Boudreau guided the
Indians to the world title.

No. 715

After months of anticipation, Henry Aaron entered the game on April 8, 1974, needing just one home run to break Babe Ruth's hallowed career record of 714. At 9:07 P.M. in Atlanta, Aaron lined a 1–0 slider from L.A.'s Al Downing over the left-center-field fence. The scoreboard blazed: "Move over, Babe, here comes Henry!" The new home run king was mobbed by his teammates as he reached home plate, where his mother gave him the biggest hug of all.

"It's more timing than anything else. You don't have to be real big. Time it right, and the ball will go far enough."

—HANK AARON ON HITTING HOMERS,
YOUNG BASEBALL CHAMPIONS

1947: Yankees vs. Dodgers

This Series matched two teams that were each beginning a string of greatness. The Yanks of Babe Ruth and Lou Gehrig were gone; in their place were Joe DiMaggio, Yogi Berra, and Phil Rizzuto. The Dodgers were about to become one of the greatest bunches in National League history. It was Jackie Robinson's first season; Pete Reiser and Pee Wee Reese were blossoming stars.

The most sensational game was the fourth, won by Brooklyn. With two out in the last of the ninth, pinch hitter Cookie Lavagetto cracked the only hit the Dodgers had all game. But it was enough to score two men who had walked, giving Brooklyn a 3–2 win. The Dodgers won Game 6 thanks to outfielder Al Gionfriddo's spectacular catch, but New York took the finale 5–2.

Al Gionfriddo

GAME 1	Brooklyn 3 at New York 5
GAME 2	Brooklyn 3 at New York 10
GAME 3	New York 8 at Brooklyn 9
GAME 4	New York 2 at Brooklyn 3
GAME 5	New York 2 at Brooklyn 1
GAME 6	Brooklyn 8 at New York 6
GAME 7	Brooklyn 2 at New York 5

"You can have it. It wouldn't do me any good."

—Ray Chapman to umpire Billy Evans after taking two strikes from Walter Johnson in 1915; he had already been on his way to the dugout when Evans informed him he still had one strike

"You can't hit what you **can't see."**

—John Daley after pinch-hitting against Walter Johnson in 1912

Walter Johnson

"I think
*the ball
disintegrated*
on the way to the
plate and the catcher
put it back together
again. I swear, when it
went past the plate it
was just the spit that
went by."
—SAM CRAWFORD ON
ED WALSH'S SPITTER

Ed Walsh

Wrigley Field, Chicago

Nestled within a charming North Side neighborhood, the Cubs' Wrigley Field lives up to its nickname "The Friendly Confines." The team's loyal fans are treated to magnificent views of Chicago, ivy-covered walls, and home runs galore—especially when the Windy City gales are blowing out. On top of the huge old-time, hand-operated scoreboard, the flags of each team fly in the order of that day's standings. During each game, a different celebrity leads fans in singing "Take Me Out to the Ballgame." While the ballpark seats just 41,118 (2006), some fans catch the action from the rooftops of condo and apartment buildings beyond the outfield fences.

Most Managerial Wins

1	Connie Mack	3,731
2	John McGraw	2,763
3	Tony LaRussa	2,296
4	Sparky Anderson	2,194
5	Bobby Cox	2,170
6	Bucky Harris	2,157
7	Joe McCarthy	2,125
8	Walter Alston	2,040
9	Leo Durocher	2,008
10	Joe Torre	1,973

Connie Mack

"Well, you *can't win them all.*"

—CONNIE MACK ON HIS 1916 A's, WHO WENT 36–117

Christy Mathewson

On major-league career lists, Mathewson ranks third in wins (373), third in shutouts (79), and eighth in ERA (2.13).

The right-handed screwballer won at least 22 games for the New York Giants for 12 consecutive seasons, including 30 or more wins in 1903, '04, '05, and '08.

In four World Series, Mathewson notched 10 complete games, including three shutouts in the 1905 season.

The clean-cut, deep-thinking college man was renowned for his intelligence, class, and fadeaway fastball. Worshipped nationwide, he was considered a fine example for a game that was cleaning up its image.

W	L	ERA	G	CG	IP	H	ER	BB	SO
373	188	2.13	635	434	4,780.2	4,218	1,133	844	2,502

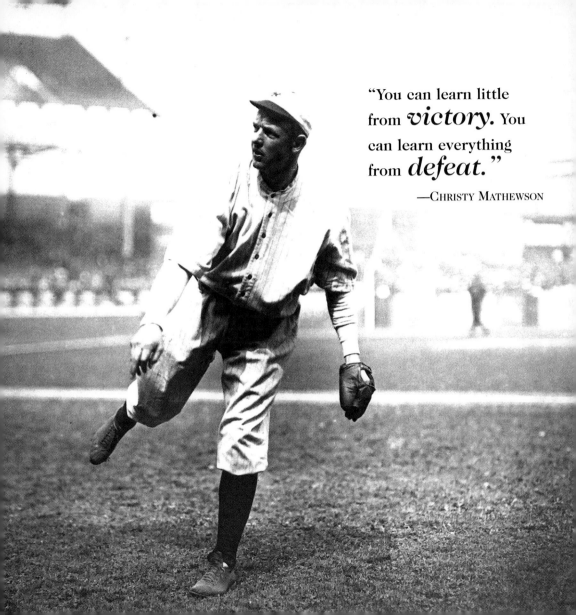

"You can learn little from *victory*. You can learn everything from *defeat*."

—CHRISTY MATHEWSON

The Last *.400* Season

In 1941 Ted Williams, the best hitter in baseball, enjoyed the greatest season of his career, flirting with .400 all year long. On Memorial Day his average was a dizzying .429; it rose as high as .438 at one point. Entering a season-ending doubleheader at Philadelphia, the Splendid Splinter was hitting .39955—technically .400. His manager offered him a chance to take the day off and claim the .400 crown, but winning a batting title while sitting on the bench was not Ted's style. He proceeded to smash six hits over the two games to finish at .406—the last .400 season by any major-league hitter.

Yankees manager Joe McCarthy won seven world championships. Known for staying seated squarely in the middle of the dugout (which he called his "command post"), he claimed never to have challenged an umpire on anything but rules and never to have gone to the mound to remove a pitcher.

"Look at it.
'World Series.
Saturday. 8 P.M.'
Nice. *That is
nice.*"

—YANKEE MANAGER JOE TORRE,
OBSERVING THE MARQUEE
OUTSIDE YANKEE STADIUM;
TORRE HAD WAITED
36 YEARS AS A PLAYER AND
MANAGER TO REACH HIS
FIRST FALL CLASSIC,
SPORTS ILLUSTRATED,
OCTOBER 28, 1996

Rodriguez caught fans' attention as a 21-year-old for Seattle in 1996, when he batted .358 with 36 homers, 123 RBI's, 54 doubles, and 141 runs.

For the Mariners in 1998, A-Rod became just the third player in history to amass 40 homers and 40 steals in the same season.

From 1998 through 2003, Alex proved to be the greatest-slugging middle infielder ever, averaging 47 home runs as a shortstop. From 2001 through 2003 with Texas, he won three straight American League home run crowns, with 57 longballs in 2002.

In 2003, Rodriguez won his first league MVP Award and his second Gold Glove Award. In 2005, he won his second American League MVP.

BA	G	AB	R	H	2B	3B	HR	RBI	SB
.305	1,746	6,767	1,358	2,067	364	26	464	1,347	241

In 2004, **Rodriguez** became the *youngest player ever* (age 28) to reach 350 home runs.

A Full Count

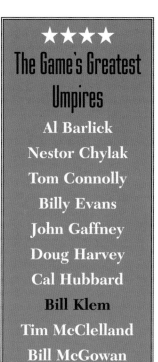

★★★★
The Game's Greatest Umpires

Al Barlick
Nestor Chylak
Tom Connolly
Billy Evans
John Gaffney
Doug Harvey
Cal Hubbard
Bill Klem
Tim McClelland
Bill McGowan

Most baseball historians agree that Bill Klem was the greatest umpire ever. In fact, he was so good at calling balls and strikes that for 16 years they *wouldn't let him umpire the bases,* putting him behind the plate for every game he refereed. For 37 years, he was the best. When Klem retired in 1941, he was put in charge of all National League umpires in hopes he would pass his skills and attitude along to them.

"It *ain't nothing* till I *call it.*"
—BILL KLEM

From a notoriety standpoint, Duke Snider played "third wheel" to fellow center field superstars Willie Mays and Mickey Mantle in New York even though he was the leading home run hitter for the decade of the '50s.

"Best one-legged player I ever saw."
—CASEY STENGEL ON OFT-INJURED MICKEY MANTLE, *BASEBALL DIGEST,* NOVEMBER 1995

The *Luckiest* Man

In 1939 Yankees slugger Lou Gehrig was diagnosed with amyotrophic lateral sclerosis, an incurable disease that would one day bear his name. On July 4 that year, *New Yorkers saluted Gehrig* in a sold-out tribute ceremony at Yankee Stadium. Tears flowed as Gehrig addressed the crowd: "Fans, for the past two weeks you have been reading about the bad break I got. Yet today I consider myself the luckiest man on the face of the earth."

Career Save Leaders

1	Trevor Hoffman	482
2	Lee Smith	478
3	John Franco	424
4	Mariano Rivera	413
5	Dennis Eckersley	390
6	Jeff Reardon	367
7	Randy Myers	347
8	Rollie Fingers	341
9	John Wetteland	330
10	Roberto Hernandez	326

Lee Smith

Classic Ballpark

SBC Park, San Francisco

Never have fans felt more alive at a ball game than at SBC Park, just a Barry Bonds home run away from San Francisco Bay—or McCovey's Cove, as it's called. Fans love watching the sailboats, and boaters enjoy watching the game. An architectural marvel, SBC Park features a neo-retro scoreboard and a gigantic Coke bottle that kids can slide down. The park is immaculate, and the food—especially the garlic fries—is delectable.

The Brooklyn Giant

If a man is measured by his reaction to challenges, Hall of Fame catcher Roy Campanella should be remembered as a giant more than a Dodger. A member of the Negro National League by the age of 15, he had to wait 10 seasons for the major-league doors to swing open to blacks. Eventually signed by Dodger President Branch Rickey, "Campy" joined fellow trailblazer Jackie Robinson in Brooklyn in 1948

> "You gotta be mean to play baseball for a living, but you gotta have a lot of little boy in you, too."
> —ROY CAMPANELLA

and became an anchor on five pennant-winning teams. Campanella was named MVP in 1951, 1953, and '55. He was a well-liked and respected clubhouse leader with a brilliant grin and infectious enthusiasm.

His career was snuffed out at age 36 by a 1958 car accident that left him a quadriplegic, but Campy never let a wheelchair dampen his zest for living. And in four ensuing decades as a Dodger instructor, coach, and community-relations manager, he touched more lives than he ever could have with a few more home runs.

"Having **Willie Stargell** on your team is like having a diamond ring on your finger."

—PITTSBURGH MANAGER CHUCK TANNER, *TIME*, OCTOBER 29, 1979

Favorite Flicks

★★★★
Best Baseball Films

The Bad News Bears (1976)
Bang the Drum Slowly (1973)
Bull Durham (1988)
Eight Men Out (1988)
Field of Dreams (1989)
A League of Their Own (1992)
Major League (1989)
The Natural (1984)
The Pride of the Yankees (1942)
The Sandlot (1993)

Who ever imagined minor-league baseball could be so sexy? In *Bull Durham*, Susan Sarandon drives aging catcher Kevin Costner and bizarre rookie pitcher Tim Robbins crazy. Unlike most baseball films, this one takes us down to the bushes, where players carry their own bags, rehearse what they'll say if they're ever interviewed, and dream of "the show."

CHAPTER FOUR

Wild Pitches & Out-of-the-Park Dingers

"The only thing that's certain is they'll play the *National Anthem* before every game."

—RICK MONDAY

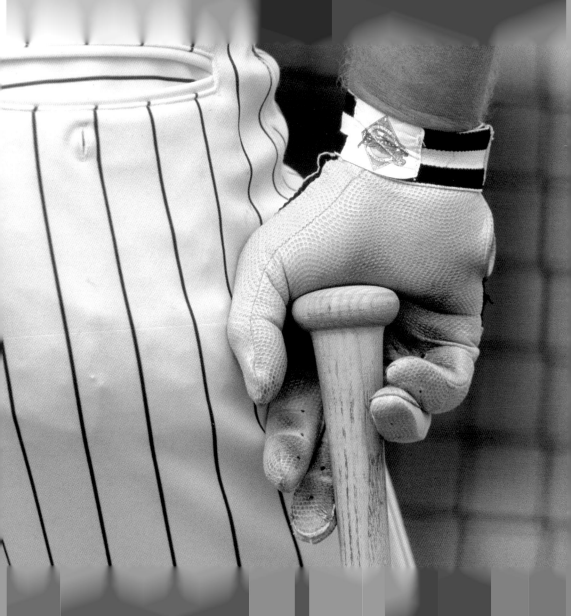

Faster than a Speeding Bullet

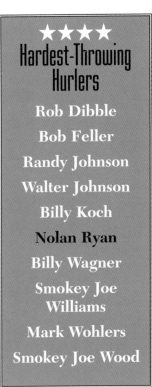

★★★★
Hardest-Throwing Hurlers

Rob Dibble
Bob Feller
Randy Johnson
Walter Johnson
Billy Koch
Nolan Ryan
Billy Wagner
Smokey Joe Williams
Mark Wohlers
Smokey Joe Wood

Nolan Ryan was an unbelievable physical phenomenon. He got even better with age: Even after age 40, he *pitched better* (and some say *faster*) than he ever had. Ryan's 100-mph fastball was matched by his incredible *discipline* and *devotion* to the game. Six times he fanned more than 300 batters in one season. Ryan tossed seven no-hitters, and he struck out 1,500 more batters than the next best pitcher.

Willie Mays

Two things made Willie Mays special: One was his absolutely unequaled collection of skills. He was a great hitter, a wonderful fielder with a super arm, a sensational slugger, and a baserunner of blazing speed and daring. Sure, for each of those talents there was someone who did it better. But no one else combined *all* of those abilities to such a degree. The other, equally magical side of his playing style was his childlike enthusiasm and love of the game. Willie wasn't beating you to show you up; he was clobbering you because it was so much *fun*. He flew out from under his cap as he ran. He chased down fly balls with not only pure speed but also genuine exuberance. His trademark greeting, "Say hey!" somehow communicated his delightful attitude.

Mays was among the last Negro Leaguers to make the majors. He emerged as a 20-year-old New York Giant in 1951. Rookie of the Year (.274, 20 homers) on the National League champions, he missed most of the next two years fulfilling military obligations. He returned in '54, rippling with new muscle and ready to wreak havoc on NL pitching, and his incredible Hall of Fame career was off and running.

Willie Mays wasn't just great, he was durable as well: His string of 13 consecutive 150-game seasons is an all-time record. Every year Willie's name was at the top of one or another statistical category: triples or homers (four times); batting or slugging average; runs, hits, or walks. He was chosen as league MVP twice. As the best of the best, it made sense that every year Willie made the All-Star Game his own personal showcase. It was a treat that fans of the era anticipated and savored. He seemed to be in the middle of every important play in the midseason classic—cracking a key double, stealing a vital base, making a critical circus catch.

Willie's over-the-shoulder catch of Vic Wertz's 430-foot smash to center in the '54 World Series has been called the greatest grab of all time, and it brought into national focus another key aspect of Mays's game: his defense.

> "The only man who could have caught it, hit it."
> —SPORTSWRITER BOB STEVENS AFTER MAYS BELTED A DRIVE OVER THE CENTER FIELDER'S HEAD

Willie won a Gold Glove each of the first 12 years in which the trophy was awarded, routinely turning in fantastic plays. He patented a flashy, one-handed basket catch, and—even with runners wary of testing his arm—recorded 12 or more assists on nine occasions.

By the time he retired he had hit more home runs (660) than anyone besides Babe Ruth. And Willie had lost two seasons to military service, too. Many baseball experts have called him the greatest player ever. Actress and baseball devotee Tallulah Bankhead once said, "There have been only two authentic geniuses in the world, Willie Mays and Willie Shakespeare." Who could argue with that?

BA	G	AB	R	H	2B	3B	HR	RBI	SB
.302	2,992	10,881	2,062	3,283	523	140	660	1,903	338

Ted Williams and Joe DiMaggio were baseball's shining stars throughout the '40s. In '49, there were reports the heavy hitters would be traded for each other, but the Yankees declined when the Red Sox wanted Yogi Berra included in the deal.

Yes, one man can turn a team around. It happened for the Mets when Tom Seaver reached the big leagues in 1967. That year, on a team that lost 101 games, he went 16–13 and earned Rookie of the Year honors. With his golden arm and spirited leadership, "Tom Terrific" transformed baseball's laughingstocks into the 1969 world champions.

Patrons paid 71 cents per Bob Gibson *strikeout* (he had 17) in Game 1 of the '68 Series.

Bob Gibson, the man many call "the ultimate big-game pitcher."

Single-Season Batting Leaders

1 Nap Lajoie   .426   1901

2 Rogers Hornsby   .424   1924

3 George Sisler   .420   1922

4 Ty Cobb   .420   1911

5 Ty Cobb   .409   1912

6 Joe Jackson   .408   1911

7 George Sisler   .407   1920

8 Ted Williams   .406   1941

9 Rogers Hornsby   .403   1925

10 Harry Heilmann   .403   1923

Nap Lajoie

The greatest player in Padres history, Tony Gwynn eclipsed 3,000 hits, won eight National League batting titles, and topped .300 for 19 consecutive seasons. His .394 average in 1994 was the best in the majors since 1941.

Maris *One-ups* the Babe

In 1961 not one but *two* men were in full rush to bust the Babe's single-season home run record—Yankee sluggers **Mickey Mantle** and **Roger Maris.** While New York's fans and reporters didn't mind if the charismatic Mantle broke the fabled Bambino's record, they gave Maris a hard time—booing him and browbeating him with questions. By late August, injuries had knocked Mantle off the pace, and he finished the season with 54 homers while Maris went on to the promised land. Despite insomnia and nightmares, *Maris persevered.* In the season's final game, *he belted No. 61* against Boston at Yankee Stadium.

While hitting a then-record *61 homers* for the New York Yankees during the *1961* season, Roger Maris never received an intentional walk; Mickey Mantle was batting behind him.

Satchel Paige

Paige, hailed as the greatest Negro League pitcher of all time, achieved such feats as 64 consecutive scoreless innings, 21 straight wins, and a 31–4 record for the Pittsburgh Crawfords in 1933.

The right-handed fireballer claimed he tossed 55 no-hitters and approximately 300 shutouts in his lifetime.

When he finally was brought to the majors in 1948, he went 6–1 with a 2.48 ERA as a 42-year-old rookie, helping the Cleveland Indians win their first world title since 1920.

In 1965, at age 59, Paige pitched three shutout innings for the Kansas City Athletics, becoming the oldest man ever to pitch in the majors.

W	L	ERA	G	CG	IP	H	ER	BB	SO
28	31	3.29	179	7	476.0	429	174	183	290

"Age is a question of mind over matter. If you don't mind, it doesn't matter."

—Satchel Paige

Walter "Red" Barber

Baseball on the Radio

They say that during summer in the 1940s, a baseball fan could walk along Flatbush Avenue in Brooklyn and never miss an inning of a Dodgers game. The radio broadcasts could be heard through the open windows of apartment buildings and local merchants. Such was the power—and magic—of baseball on the radio.

Red Barber, Mel Allen, Jack Buck, Vin Scully, and Ernie Harwell were some of the great announcers as the golden age of radio and baseball meshed. Their voices filled homes throughout each summer as they became the daily companions of the true baseball fan. Even today, many fans still recall their greatest baseball memories in the way in which the radio broadcasters described them.

Yankee Stadium, New York

Christened by Babe Ruth with a home run in 1923 and forever since known as "The House that Ruth Built," Yankee Stadium is still the place to visit to bask in baseball history. Over the years, the park has hosted 33 World Series, with the Bronx Bombers prevailing in 26 of them. The stadium's signature features include a short porch in right, "Death Valley" in left-center, and monuments of five pinstriped legends beyond the outfield fence: Ruth, Lou Gehrig, Joe DiMaggio, Mickey Mantle, and manager Miller Huggins.

No Excuses

"I wanted to be like Nolan Ryan. I didn't want to be like Pete Gray." Such were the boyhood dreams of Jim Abbott, who sought a baseball career despite having a right arm that ended just above the wrist. Abbott had no intention of making the majors as an oddity. He yearned to succeed on his talent alone, and in the end he would do so—but not without becoming a reluctant hero.

Abbott taught himself to transfer his glove from his left arm to his right by throwing against a brick wall. He later said that his missing hand "wasn't really an issue when I was a kid." By becoming an expert fielder, he kept hitters from using the logical tactic of bunting against him to their advantage. During his college career he racked up a 26–8 record at the University of Michigan, took home the Sullivan Award in 1987 as the nation's best amateur athlete, and won a gold medal in the 1988 Olympics.

California's No. 1 pick in the 1988 draft, Abbott became one of a handful of players in history to completely bypass the minor leagues, then overcame a media circus to go 12–12 as a rookie with the 1989 Angels. More great moments would follow—including a 1993 no-hitter for the Yankees—and it wasn't long before he had gotten his wish. He was simply Jim Abbott—pitcher.

"To know for sure, I'd have to **throw with a normal hand,** and I've never tried it."
—MORDECAI "THREE FINGER" BROWN, WHEN ASKED IF HIS CURVEBALL WAS AIDED BY THE MANGLED FINGERS ON HIS PITCHING HAND

Sealing the Deal

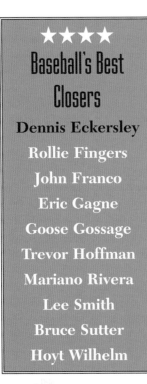

★★★★
Baseball's Best Closers

Dennis Eckersley
Rollie Fingers
John Franco
Eric Gagne
Goose Gossage
Trevor Hoffman
Mariano Rivera
Lee Smith
Bruce Sutter
Hoyt Wilhelm

Personal problems kept Dennis Eckersley from stardom as a starting pitcher during his first 12 years in the majors. But he put his demons behind him and moved into the bullpen, where he can lay claim to being the greatest closer ever. From 1988 to '92, he rang up 220 saves and 24 wins with just nine losses, and he struck out 378 while walking only 38. In 1989 and '90 combined, *he amassed more saves* (81) than hits allowed (73)—and he walked just seven batters!

Walter Johnson

The Cy Young Award is given annually to the best pitcher in each league, which is ironic considering it isn't even named for the finest pitcher of all time. Sure, Young had more wins than any major-leaguer with 511. But as Cy's time was winding down around 1910, another hurler was just getting started with the old Washington Senators. And before he was through 21 years later, Walter Perry Johnson would be heralded as one of the game's grandest gentlemen—and the greatest pitcher of them all.

The son of Kansas farmers, Johnson was discovered playing for a semipro team in Idaho and was dispatched on a train to Washington—and the major leagues. A long-limbed right-hander with an easy delivery, the 19-year-old

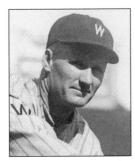

could throw a 100-mph fastball. He struggled to learn on the job, however, going 32–48 over his first three years with teams that never rose above seventh place.

More comfortable with his role as Washington's ace by 1910, Johnson had his first spectacular season with a 25–17 record, 1.35 ERA, and 313 strikeouts for the seventh-place Senators. In a pattern that would repeat itself many times, the man nicknamed "Big Train" after the freewheeling locomotives of his day was a frequent victim of nonsupport from his light-hitting mates. He eventually would amass a record 64 contests decided by a 1–0 score—winning 38 of them.

The Senators showed dramatic improvement over the next few years, and Johnson anchored second-place finishes in 1912 and '13 with records of 33–12 and 36–7. The latter season may have been the finest performance ever by a major-league hurler. It included such glittering numbers as a 1.14 ERA, 11 shutouts, and five one-hitters. Those who claim Sandy Koufax's 1962–66 binge was the finest five-year stretch in history should view Johnson's work from 1912 to '16: a 149–70 record, an ERA below 1.90 each season, 1,202 strikeouts, and just 326 walks over 1,794 innings. Eventually, Johnson would pace the AL 12 times in strikeouts, six times in wins, and five times in ERA.

Washington slipped back to the second division as the years wore on, finishing with a winning record in just four seasons from 1914 to '23. Walter still put together six consecutive 20-win campaigns during those years, and then, at age 36, enjoyed the most satisfying year of his career: In 1924 he led the league with a 23–7 record, 2.72 ERA, and 158 strikeouts, then capped it off by winning the seventh game of the only victorious World Series in Senators history.

Two more seasons and another World Series appearance remained before a broken leg derailed Johnson's career, but by then he had racked up 417 wins (second only to Young), a 2.17 ERA, and 3,509 strikeouts (a record that stood for more than 50 years). Shutouts? Johnson compiled a record 110 of them, 34 more than a guy named Young.

> "You can't hit what you can't see."
> —JOHN DALEY OF THE ST. LOUIS BROWNS
> AFTER PINCH-HITTING AGAINST JOHNSON

W	L	ERA	G	CG	IP	H	ER	BB	SO
417	279	2.17	802	531	5,923.0	4,927	1,424	1,362	3,509

Gibson's *Pinch-hit* Heroics

Due to injuries to both legs, Dodgers slugger Kirk Gibson didn't dress for Game 1 of the 1988 World Series. But when L.A. fell behind Oakland 4–3, the team's heart and soul slipped on his uniform. With one on and two outs in the bottom of the ninth, he limped to the plate. Lunging at a Dennis Eckersley pitch, Gibson willed the ball over the right-field fence. A nation looked on in amazement as Gibson limped around the bases, pumping his fist in victory.

"Nobody is half as good as Mickey Mantle."

—AL KALINE RESPONDING TO A YOUNG BOY
WHO HAD SAID TO HIM, "YOU'RE NOT
HALF AS GOOD AS MICKEY MANTLE."

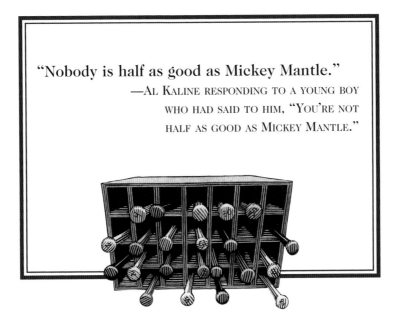

Notable Nicknames

Jimmy "Foxy Grandpa" Bannon

Bill "Ding Dong" Bell

Mordecai "Three Finger" Brown

Buttermilk Tommy Dowd

Piccolo Pete Elko

Phil "Scrap Iron" Garner

Doug "Eyechart" Gwosdz

Mike "The Human Rain
    Delay" Hargrove - - - - - - - - - - -

Charlie "Piano Legs" Hickman ─┐

Shoeless Joe Jackson

Bill "Baby Doll" Jacobson

Willie "Puddin' Head" Jones

Wee Willie Keeler - - - - - - - ┐

Mark "Humpty Dumpty" Polhemus

Jimmy "The Human Mosquito"
    Slagle

Career Win Leaders

1   Cy Young   511

2   Walter Johnson   417

3   Grover Alexander   373

    Christy Mathewson   373

5   Pud Galvin   364

6   Warren Spahn   363

7   Kid Nichols   361

8   Roger Clemens   348

9   Tim Keefe   342

10   Greg Maddux   333

Grover Alexander

The stellar performance of **Warren Spahn** and **Johnny Sain** in 1948 fueled the Braves' drive to the pennant. During one September stretch the duo started 11 of 16 games, going 9–2. *"Spahn and Sain and pray for rain"* was the rallying cry.

Warren Spahn (left) *and Johnny Sain*

Lefty Grove

Grove, who amassed 300 wins with the Philadelphia A's and Boston Red Sox, ended his career with a .680 winning percentage—the best of any 300-game winner in baseball.

The temperamental hurler won the AL "pitching triple crown" in both 1930 (28–5, 2.54 ERA, 209 strikeouts) and 1931 (31–4, 2.06, 175), and he captured nine ERA crowns, more than any other pitcher in history.

From 1928 to 1933, a golden era for hitters, Ol' Mose went 152–41 with a 2.67 ERA. In 1931 he took home the AL MVP crown.

W	L	ERA	G	CG	IP	H	ER	BB	SO
300	141	3.06	616	298	3,940.2	3,849	1,339	1,187	2,266

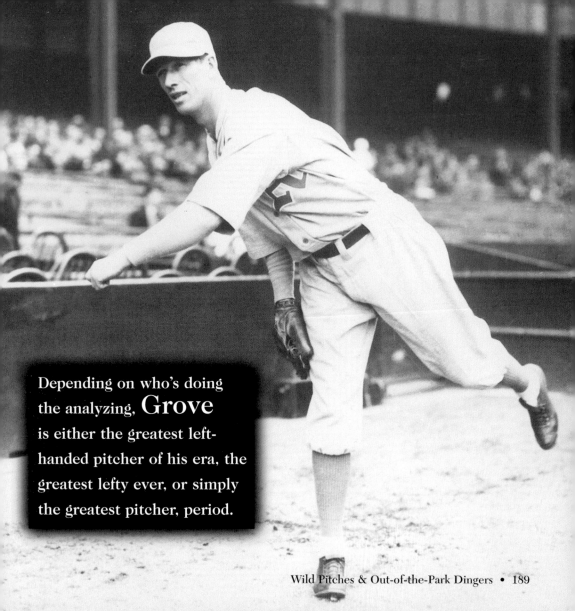

Depending on who's doing the analyzing, **Grove** is either the greatest left-handed pitcher of his era, the greatest lefty ever, or simply the greatest pitcher, period.

In a publicity stunt hatched by Browns owner Bill Veeck, 43-inch, 65-pound Eddie Gaedel emerged out of a cake wearing uniform number ⅛ and was sent up to pinch-hit against the Tigers on August 19, 1951. Batting out of a crouch, he was walked on four straight pitches.

"BROUGHT JACKIE ROBINSON TO BROOKLYN IN 1947."
—Final line on Branch Rickey's Hall of Fame plaque

1955: Dodgers vs. Yankees

The Yankees had topped the Brooklyn Dodgers in 1949, and the Dodgers narrowly missed reaching the Series in 1950 and '51. When the two teams went head to head in 1952 and '53, the story was the same: Yanks won.

But the 1955 Dodgers had a new manager, Walter Alston, and a new set of heroes. Duke Snider clubbed four homers in the Series, a feat only Babe Ruth, Lou Gehrig, and Snider himself had previously accomplished. Pitcher Roger Craig stifled the Yanks in Game 5. Johnny Podres won Games 3 and 7. In the Series finale, the Dodgers were hanging on to a 2–0 lead when Sandy Amoros— brought into the game for defensive purposes—made an impossible grab of a tailing Yogi Berra liner and turned a potentially game-tying double into a double play. "Next year" finally had arrived in Brooklyn.

GAME 1	Brooklyn 5 at New York 6		GAME 5	New York 3 at Brooklyn 5
GAME 2	Brooklyn 2 at New York 4		GAME 6	Brooklyn 1 at New York 5
GAME 3	New York 3 at Brooklyn 8		GAME 7	Brooklyn 2 at New York 0
GAME 4	New York 5 at Brooklyn 8			

When he was signed by the Giants at age 19, Juan Marichal, the "Dominican Dandy," brought with him a curve, a slider, a screwball, and a lightning-quick fastball. He threw them all with pinpoint control and, of course, his trademark high kick.

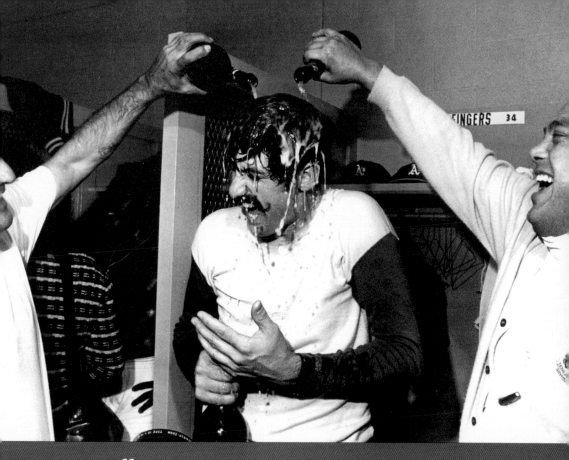

Rollie Fingers got a well-deserved celebratory champagne dousing after saving the clincher in the 1972 World Series against Cincinnati.

Honus Wagner

Often mentioned alongside Ty Cobb as one of the greatest players of the dead-ball era, John Peter Wagner could not have been more different from his contemporary. The pride of the Pirates was a notorious Mr. Nice  Guy, as modest and even-tempered as Terrible Ty was vicious and bullheaded. Most famous these days as the guy whose 1910 baseball card could pay for a new house and college education, "The Flying Dutchman" also happened to be a .327 lifetime hitter with a National League–record eight batting titles and 722 stolen bases—as well as the greatest-fielding shortstop this side of Ozzie Smith.

Supposedly discovered tossing coal chunks at a boxcar near his tiny Penn- sylvania hometown, Honus joined Louisville of the NL as an outfielder in 1897. Squat (5′11″, 200 pounds) and bowlegged with a long, beaked nose, Wagner didn't look like a ballplayer—until he got on a field. Once there, the right-handed, barrel-chested slug- ger with deceptive speed hit .299 and .336 his first two full seasons, with more than 100 RBI per year.

The Louisville franchise shifted to his hometown of Pittsburgh in 1900, and Wagner celebrated by collecting his first NL batting title with a career-high .381 mark while leading the NL in doubles (45), triples (22), and slugging (.573). League leader in RBI (126 and 91) and stolen bases (49 and 42) each of the next two seasons, he hit .353 and

.330 as the Pirates won back-to-back NL championships.

After playing as many as five positions in a season, Wagner thrived once he was named Pittsburgh's starting shortstop in 1903. Becoming the game's best fielder at the spot, he developed a rifle arm and used his huge hands to scoop up everything hit near him. He also hit .350 with seven batting titles over the next nine seasons, earning the first in '03 when he hit .355 with 101 RBI, 46 steals, and a league-high 19 triples to power the Pirates to their third straight pennant.

Never hitting more than 10 home runs, Wagner paced the league in slugging six times as the classic dead-ball power hitter—leading the NL seven times in doubles, collecting 10 or more triples 13 times, and notching 100 or more RBI on nine occasions, leading the league five times. Stolen-base king five times, he swiped 40 or more eight straight years.

Retiring at age 43 as the National League leader in hits (3,415), runs (1,736), doubles (640), and triples (252), the charter Hall of Famer still ranks high on each list. He came back at age 59 to coach for the Pirates and stayed on 18 years, spinning many a yarn about the good ol' days and keeping himself young.

> "There is something Lincolnesque about him, his rugged homeliness, his simplicity, his integrity, and his true nobility of character."
>
> —SPORTSWRITER ARTHUR DALE ON WAGNER

MAJOR LEAGUE TOTALS									
BA	G	AB	R	H	2B	3B	HR	RBI	SB
.327	2,792	10,430	1,736	3,415	640	252	101	1,732	722

Only one no-hitter has been pitched on Opening Day: a 1–0 win by Cleveland's Bob Feller against the Chicago White Sox on April 16, 1940. Feller was probably harmed more than any other great pitcher by World War II. While serving in the Navy, Rapid Robert lost more than four full seasons— just as he was entering his prime.

"He says *hello* on opening day and *good-bye* on closing day, and in between he *hits* *.350.*"

—MICKEY COCHRANE ON
CHARLIE GEHRINGER

Charlie Gehringer

Playing with Power

In 1998, Mark McGwire shook the baseball world by blasting 70 home runs. And he did it with power, driving 47 of his long balls 400 feet or more. Five of those blasts exceeded 500 feet, including a 545-foot bomb at St. Louis' Busch Stadium that prompted the team to slap a giant bandage on the spot it hit. The massive slugger averaged a home run every 10.6 at-bats in his career—a big-league record.

Strongest Sluggers

Jimmie Foxx
Josh Gibson
Harmon Killebrew
Dave Kingman
Mickey Mantle
Willie McCovey
Mark McGwire
Babe Ruth
Willie Stargell
Jim Thome

In 1965, **Sandy Koufax** *(left)* and **Don Drysdale** *(right)* accounted for 49 of the Dodgers' 97 wins, including *(here, postgame)* a pennant-clincher by Koufax over the Braves on October 2.

An eight-time 20-game winner for Baltimore, Jim Palmer consistently outsmarted hitters. Though he often pitched high in the strike zone, he rarely allowed a home run. In fact, he never gave up a grand slam in his entire 20-year career.

History's Hardest Thrower

The radar gun is a relatively modern device. Before its addition to the briefcase of major-league scouts and coaches, the most common way to judge speed was simply by watching the pitchers throw. Efforts were made to find more accurate measurements—Bob Feller raced his fastball against a motorcycle—but most often the judgment of batters and scouts carried the most weight. And in the eyes of those who saw Feller, Nolan Ryan, and every other hard thrower of the past half-century, the fastest of them all was Steve Dalkowski.

His name doesn't ring a bell for most fans, because he never spent a day in the majors. Through nine seasons in the Orioles organization, he struggled with horrible wildness. He averaged an incredible 13 strikeouts and 13 walks per nine innings. Year

after year, in nine different minor leagues, the left-hander toiled while Baltimore management waited for him to turn it around. The numbers were amazing—262 strikeouts and 262 walks in 170 innings during 1960, 283 pitches thrown in one game. Legends grew about the time he tore the ear off a batter with one pitch and shattered an umpire's mask with another. In 1964, his control suddenly improved and he was given a serious look by the Orioles in spring training. He blew a pitch by recently retired Ted Williams, who said simply, "Fastest ever." Then, weeks away from making the big club, Dalkowski's arm went dead without warning on a routine throw to first. It never came around, and 20 years later he was a cotton-picker by day and a hanger-on at minor-league ballparks by night—just another face in the crowd.

With a blistering 100-mph fastball, Randy Johnson *shattered bats* and once even accidentally *exploded a bird* in flight. From 1997 through 2002, he went 120–42, averaged 340 strikeouts, and won four Cy Young Awards.

CHAPTER FIVE

Grand Slams & Grandstanding

"If you're not *having fun* [in baseball], you miss the point of everything."

—CHRIS CHAMBLISS

Personality Plus

Yogi Berra's marvelous, sometimes uproarious, nearly Zen (but not quite) *"Yogi-isms"* are inextricably intertwined with baseball lore. These bons mots often showcase a mind with a keen understanding of the game. Not many people remember that the Yankees catcher who pronounced the deep truth about baseball—*"It ain't over till it's over"*—left the historic third game of the 1951 National League playoffs in the eighth inning.

"I want to *thank everyone* who made this day necessary."
—YOGI BERRA, ADDRESSING THE ST. LOUIS CROWD ON YOGI BERRA APPRECIATION DAY

Stengelese

The lexicon of baseball is filled with catchy phrases. A lazy fly ball is known as a "can of a corn." A double play is often described as a "twin killing," and runners on base are also known as "ducks on the pond." But for decades Casey Stengel and Yogi Berra spoke their own brand of baseball language. They were masters of the malaprop and the mixed metaphor. When Casey went on a rant, it was known as *Stengelese.* When Berra offered advice, it was a *Yogi-ism.*

Stengel managed his share of miserable teams, including the 1934–36 Dodgers, 1938–43 Braves, and 1962–65 Mets. But his legacy also includes the 1949–60 New York Yankees, whom he managed to ten pennants. During this time he became known as the "Old Perfessor." Warren Spahn pitched for Stengel with both the Braves and the Mets, prompting him to note that he played for Casey "both before and after he was a genius."

Classic Stengelese

Stengel called rookies "green peas," a good fielder was a "plumber," and a tough ballplayer was someone who could "squeeze your earbrows off."

"Good pitching will always stop good hitting and vice versa."

"I don't know if he throws a spitball, but he sure spits on the ball."

"Being with a woman all night never hurt no professional baseball player. It's staying up all night looking for a woman that does him in."

Casey Stengel (left) *with Yogi Berra*

Mickey Mantle

The New York Yankees all but ruled baseball from 1920 to 1964, and Mickey was the last representative of the line of superheroes who anchored the team: Ruth, Gehrig, DiMaggio... and the Mick. Before his

hitter from Commerce, Oklahoma, Mantle overcame a bone disease in his left leg to make the Yankees as a 19-year-old outfielder in 1951. He recovered from a tough start to deliver a fine rookie year dimmed only by

rookie season, manager Casey Stengel, usually wisely circumspect when stating a player's skills, was unequivocal about the kid's prospects. "He should lead the league in everything. With his combination of power and speed he should win the triple batting crown every year. In fact, he should do everything he wants to do."

Mickey Charles Mantle was something special indeed: an amazing combination of power, speed, and presence; the golden boy of New York (and all of baseball, for that matter). A switch-

an injury to his good leg sustained in the Yankees' World Series win over the Giants. It was just the start of the health hazards that would plague Mantle's career. But as the starting center fielder on the most dominating team in baseball history, Mantle's star rose quickly. He batted .311 his second season, and he led the American League with 37 home runs in 1955.

Superb defense, blistering power (the term "tape-measure home run" was coined after his 565-foot shot at Washington), and annual totals of 100-

plus runs and 90-plus RBI were not enough for some fans awaiting the next DiMaggio. Only after putting together an MVP/ Triple Crown season in 1956 (pacing the league with a .353 aver-age, 52 homers, 130 RBI, 132 runs, and .705 slugging percentage) did Mantle win everyone over. He cracked a career-high .365 with 34 home runs to cop a second straight Most Valuable Player trophy in '57, and in 1961 he waged a season-long assault against Babe Ruth's record of 60 homers. He wound up six short when he was side-lined in September by a hip infection, and teammate Roger Maris then heard the booing not only for challenging Ruth, but also for outdoing Mantle.

> "He is the kind of ballplayer who is so good...it makes everybody want to follow his example."
> —ELSTON HOWARD ON LONGTIME YANKEE TEAMMATE MICKEY MANTLE

When he recovered to win a third MVP prize in '62 (.321–30–89), many still thought he might challenge Ruth's all-time record of 714 homers. But injuries (including surgery on one shoulder and both legs) and years of hard drinking had worn down his body, and after a strong year in '64 capped by three World Series home runs (his 18 homers in 12 Series broke Ruth's record), he and the Yankees began a rapid decline. After hitting just .237 in 1968, he quit in disgust at age 37.

Mantle's 536 homers, 1,509 RBI, and leadership on seven World Series champions guaranteed him a Hall of Fame plaque, but his perseverance alone became legendary.

BA	G	AB	R	H	2B	3B	HR	RBI	SB
.298	2,401	8,102	1,677	2,415	344	72	536	1,509	153

Career Strikeout Leaders

1	Nolan Ryan	5,714
2	Roger Clemens	4,604
3	Randy Johnson	4,544
4	Steve Carlton	4,136
5	Bert Blyleven	3,701
6	Tom Seaver	3,640
7	Don Sutton	3,574
8	Gaylord Perry	3,534
9	Walter Johnson	3,509
10	Phil Niekro	3,342

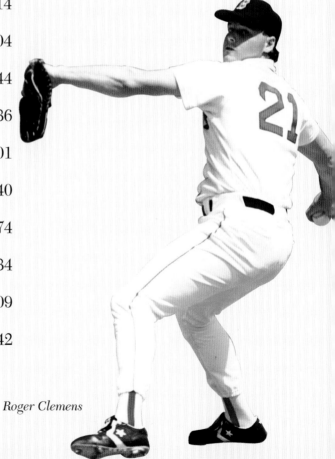

Roger Clemens

"I pitched 874 major-league *games* in 22 years, and I never had a sore arm until the day I quit. My arm went bad in 1912 when I was in spring training, and I guess it was about time."
—CY YOUNG, *BASEBALL DIGEST,*
OCTOBER 1943

1962: Yankees vs. Giants

Ralph Terry *(right)*, who had allowed the Bill Mazeroski homer that ended the 1960 Series in such dramatic fashion, redeemed himself in the taut 1962 fall classic. For six games, the New York Yankees and San Francisco Giants jabbed at each other like testy prizefighters, neither able to establish dominance. Nobody on either team homered more than once or scored more than a handful of runs.

By the time Game 7 rolled around, each team's ace starter (Jack Sanford for the Giants, Terry for the Yanks) had won one and lost one game. They faced off against each other, and it wasn't over until Giants slugger Willie McCovey drilled a line drive up the middle with two on and two out in the last of the ninth with the Yanks up 1–0—a line drive that second baseman Bobby Richardson snared to end the game.

GAME 1	New York 6 at San Francisco 2	GAME 5	San Francisco 3 at New York 5
GAME 2	New York 0 at San Francisco 2	GAME 6	New York 2 at San Francisco 5
GAME 3	San Francisco 2 at New York 3	GAME 7	New York 1 at San Francisco 0
GAME 4	San Francisco 7 at New York 3		

"Only if she were digging in."

—EARLY WYNN,
NOTORIOUS BRUSHBACK
PITCHER, ON WHETHER
HE WOULD USE SUCH
TACTICS ON HIS OWN
MOTHER

Traded for a Fence

Hall of Famer Lefty Grove got his start in the majors when he *was traded for a center-field fence.* The standout southpaw belonged to the Martinsburg, West Virginia, team when Jack Dunn, owner of the minor-league Baltimore Orioles, spotted him. Dunn learned that Martinsburg owed money for the erection of an outfield fence and offered to pay the bill in exchange for Grove. The pitcher went on to star for Baltimore before winning 300 games in the majors.

Reggie! Reggie! *Reggie!*

Charismatic slugger Reggie Jackson brought excitement to the Bronx in 1977, but Yankee fans were more interested in a world championship—which they hadn't experienced in 15 years. Jackson took care of that in Game 6 of the World Series against Los Angeles. Incredibly, he belted three home runs on three swings, the last being a 450-foot bomb to right field amid chants of "Reggie! Reggie! Reggie!" The Game 6 dramatics of "Mr. October" clinched the world title.

The Doubleday Myth

When a 1907 commission formed by A. G. Spalding set out to prove the true origins of baseball, there was little mention of previous versions of bat-and-ball games amidst patriotic praise for the supposed architect of "America's Game"—Major General Abner Doubleday. The story went that Doubleday, as a Cooperstown, New York, youngster in 1839, had drawn up a diagram of a diamond for a game he called "Town Ball." Conveniently, Doubleday later went on to heroics as the soldier who spotted the first gun fired at Fort Sumter, and was supposedly at Abraham Lincoln's deathbed when the president leaned over and whispered in his ear, "Abner, don't . . . let . . . baseball . . . die."

A great story but merely a myth—especially considering Doubleday was actually at West Point in 1839 and was never known to even follow the game he supposedly invented.

Alexander Joy Cartwright, a New York bank teller and talented draftsman, was the first to suggest teams of nine players, equidistant bases, and three outs per inning. Today, Cartwright's Hall of Fame plaque credits him as "the Father of Modern Base Ball," while Abner Doubleday, the man responsible for the placement of the Hall of Fame in Cooperstown, has himself never been enshrined.

Baseball commissioner **Judge Kenesaw Mountain Landis** showed no mercy for those Chicago White Sox who accepted money for throwing the 1919 World Series. Landis *kicked eight "Black Sox" out* of major-league baseball, including some who may have been innocent.

Ken Griffey, Jr., was named Player of the Decade for the 1990s by his fellow major-leaguers. A .300 hitter who could fly, Junior also won 10 Gold Glove Awards in the decade while blasting 382 home runs.

Nearly three months after Jackie Robinson broke baseball's color barrier, Larry Doby became the first African American to play in the American League. In 13 big-league seasons, Doby was a seven-time All-Star who hit at least 25 homers five times and drove in 100-plus runs five times.

Rickey Henderson

The top basestealer of all time, Henderson is the only major-leaguer to steal more than 1,000 bases.

"The Man of Steal" reached 100 steals for Oakland three times in the 1980s, including an ML-record 130 in 1982.

His 1,406 steals, 2,295 runs scored, and 297 homers are a Hall of Fame combination that may never be matched.

Henderson first caught fans' attention in 1977, when he *stole 95 bases*—including seven in one game—in the California League.

BA	G	AB	R	H	2B	3B	HR	RBI	SB
.279	3,081	10,961	2,295	3,055	510	66	297	1,115	1,406

Notable Nicknames

Emil "Hill Billy" Bildilli

George "Bingo Binks" Binkowski

Paul "Motormouth" Blair

Dennis "Oil Can" Boyd

Ron "The Penguin" Cey

Ron "Louisiana Lightning" Guidry

Reggie "Mr. October" Jackson - - - - - - - - - - - - - - ┐

Slothful Bill Lattimore

Sudden Sam McDowell

Hugh "Losing Pitcher" Mulcahy

John "Blue Moon" Odom

Charlie "The Old Woman in the Red Cap" Pabor

Lou "The Nervous Greek" Skizas

Frank "Sweet Music" Viola - - - - - - - - - - - - ┐

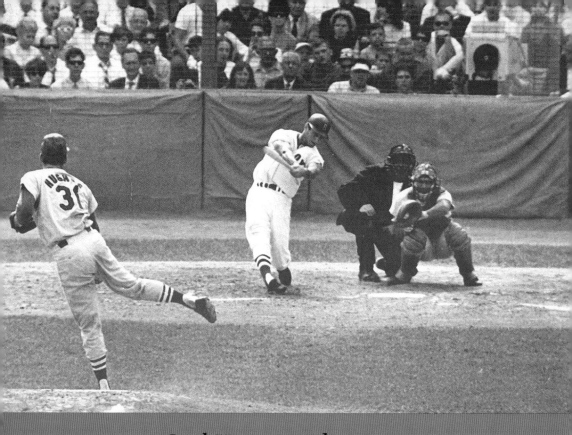

Boston star Carl Yastrzemski carried the Red Sox to the 1967 World Series by *delivering crucial hits* and making *game-saving catches.* During the last two weeks of the season he batted .523 with five homers and 16 RBI.

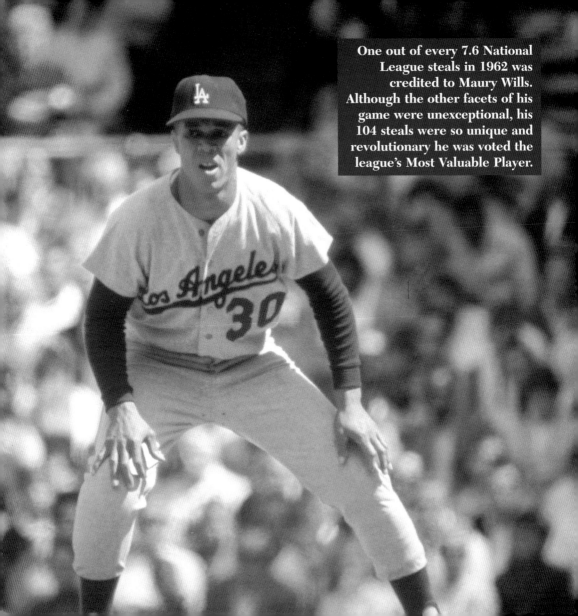

One out of every 7.6 National League steals in 1962 was credited to Maury Wills. Although the other facets of his game were unexceptional, his 104 steals were so unique and revolutionary he was voted the league's Most Valuable Player.

The Babe's *Called Shot*

The '32 World Series between the Cubs and Yankees was one of the nastiest of all time. With the Yanks leading two games to none, Chicago fans were all over the Babe when the Yanks arrived in Chicago for Game 3. Ruth came to bat in the fifth with the score tied at 4 and the bases empty. What happened next lies somewhere between myth and legend. Some say that after two strikes the Babe pointed toward center field, indicating that's where the next pitch was heading. Others say Babe just kind of waved toward the outfield, or toward the Cub bench, with his bat. Everyone agrees on what happened next. Babe smoked a line drive deep into the center-field stands, then circled the bases, laughing. Fans still debate whether the gesture meant that he had called his shot. Either way, as Ruth later said, "It makes a hell of a story, doesn't it?"

PETCO Park, San Diego

The stucco-walled PETCO Park opened in 2004 to glowing reviews. Upon entering the ballpark, Padres fans pass by a palm court, jacaranda trees, and water walls. Once inside, they're treated to views of the city skyline and other fascinating sites beyond the outfield fence, including a "beach" and a "park" for fans to enjoy. The four-story Western Metal Supply building, part of the left-field wall, has been transformed into luxury suites, a restaurant, and rooftop seating for 800 lucky fans.

Career Home Run Leaders

1	Hank Aaron	755
2	Barry Bonds	734
3	Babe Ruth	714
4	Willie Mays	660
5	Sammy Sosa	588
6	Frank Robinson	586
7	Mark McGwire	583
8	Harmon Killebrew	573
9	Rafael Palmeiro	569
10	Reggie Jackson	563
	Ken Griffey, Jr.	563

Hank Aaron

Harmon Killebrew was the son of a professional wrestler and the grandson of a man said to be the strongest soldier in the Union Army during the Civil War. "Killer," a big-leaguer at 18, muscled up for 573 home runs over 22 seasons.

Barry Bonds

Although everyone knew Barry Bonds was an outstanding ballplayer (he won three Most Valuable Player Awards before he turned 30 and was named Player of the Decade for the 1990s), in 2001 he took his game to a whole new level. He since

has elbowed his way into consideration along with Babe Ruth and Willie Mays as the greatest player of all time.

Bonds has won seven MVP Awards; no other baseball player has won more than three. In 2001 he became only the second hitter to top 70 homers in a season, belting a record 73. That season he also broke Ruth's 80-year slugging percentage standard with an .863 mark. The next year, the Giants slugger toppled Ted Williams's 60-year-old on-base percentage record, finishing with .582

thanks to 198 walks. Amazingly, he broke his own records in 2004 with 232 walks and a .609 on-base percentage. It can be said that his incredible level of batting skill has rendered him the first player in a century to change the way the game is played. Opposing managers almost steadfastly refuse to give him good pitches to hit, so he sets walks records while fans, understandably, boo. Not only is he first all time in walks received, but he has over 300 more intentional walks than the next person on the list.

Bonds continued his extraordinary play in 2004 despite turning 40 in midseason. He has maintained his lightning-quick swing, thanks to a grueling off-season conditioning program he has stuck to throughout his career. His impressive stolen-base success from 1999 through 2004—61 of 72 (85 percent)—indicates that he hadn't lost a step.

Just reviewing his batting feats can leave one breathless. Bonds is one of three people to achieve 40 homers and 40 steals in one season. He has five 30/30 seasons; the only other player to amass that many is his father, Bobby. He is the only member of the 500/500 club—and there is no one in the 400/400 club. He holds the major-league record for consecutive seasons with 30 or more homers (13). Only Babe Ruth has totaled more multi-homer games than Bonds. Today, he is mounting an attack on Hank Aaron's lifetime home run record, and many believe he will topple it.

> "The rest of us play in the major leagues. He's at another level."
> —FORMER SAN FRANCISCO GIANT RICH AURILIA ON BONDS

Despite his accomplishments, Bonds is not a beloved national hero—at least not at the level of modern-day sluggers Mark McGwire and Sammy Sosa. Barry has been called self-centered by teammates and fans, and in 2003 he was accused of using steroids, a charge he denied.

What many people don't know is that Bonds is one of baseball's great philanthropists, establishing such educational programs as Link n' Learn and the Bonds Private School Scholarship Fund. The bottom line, however, is that Bonds will be remembered for his achievements, which rank among the finest in baseball history.

BA	G	AB	R	H	2B	3B	HR	RBI	SB
.299	2,860	9,507	2,152	2,841	587	77	734	1,930	509

Manager John McGraw won more games than anyone except Connie Mack. The next nearest manager is more than 500 victories behind him. He knew what it took to win, and he made his players obey—or else. As a result, he was feared and he was hated, but he was never ignored.

Earl Weaver

is considered one of
the greatest managers
of all time. A
visionary strategist
and incendiary
competitor, he
disdained "small-ball"
strategies, not even
instituting a sign for
the hit-and-run play.
In 17 seasons, he
skippered Baltimore
to six division crowns,
four pennants, and
the 1970 World
Series title.

Pete Rose

Baseball's all-time hit leader (4,256), Rose surpassed Ty Cobb's major-league record in 1985—a record that had stood for 57 years.

"Charlie Hustle" ranks first on all-time lists in games played and at-bats, second in doubles, and fifth in runs scored.

He compiled the longest hitting streak in modern National League history (44 games) in 1978 and topped .300 15 times throughout his career.

The 17-time All-Star and 1973 league MVP was considered the heart and soul of Cincinnati's Big Red Machine.

Despite his having bested Cobb's career hit mark, Rose's spot in the Hall of Fame remains empty due to his implication in a gambling scandal.

BA	G	AB	R	H	2B	3B	HR	RBI	SB
.303	3,562	14,053	2,165	4,256	746	135	160	1,314	198

"I'd walk
through hell
in a gasoline suit to
play baseball."
—PETE ROSE

Fisk's Late-night *Heroics*

Game 6 of the 1975 World Series, Cincinnati at Boston, has been called the greatest game ever played. After Boston's Bernie Carbo tied it at 6–6 with a homer in the eighth, outfielders George Foster (Reds) and Dwight Evans (Red Sox) each prevented scores with spectacular double plays. At 12:34 A.M., in the 12th inning, Boston's Carlton Fisk pulled a high fly ball down the left-field line, then frantically tried to "wave" it fair. Almost unbelievably, the ball hit the foul pole and bounced fair, winning the game. Elation rocked through Red Sox land; this was as good as it got. The joy in Boston lasted just one day, however, as the Reds prevailed in Game 7.

"Above anything else,
I hate to lose."
—JACKIE ROBINSON,
GIANTS OF BASEBALL

"If I had *one*
wish in the
world today, it
would be that
Jackie Robinson
could be here to
see this happen."
—Frank Robinson on
being made the first
black manager in
major-league history

From August 28, 2002, to July 5, 2004, it was *"Game Over"* for Dodger opponents whenever **Eric Gagne** strode to the mound. Gagne racked up a record 84 saves in 84 opportunities in that time, striking out 207 and giving up only 71 hits. His ERA was an almost-unbelievable 0.82. Not surprisingly, he took home the NL Cy Young Award in '03.

"He's the only guy I know who can go 4-for-3."
—WHITE SOX INFIELDER ALAN BARRISTER ON ROD CAREW

1972: Athletics vs. Reds

It was the new wave versus the old guard: the long-haired, mustachioed Oakland A's against the clean-cropped, all-American Cincinnati Reds. Dick Williams managed Charlie Finley's wild brigade; Cincy manager Sparky Anderson headed up the Big Red Machine.

By the time they were finished, every game but one had been decided by one run. Reds superstar Johnny Bench, in the midst of an intentional walk on a 3–2 pitch, watched strike three zip past him. Oakland's Gene Tenace, with four homers, established himself as one of the Series' unexpected heroes. A's closer Rollie Fingers preserved a 3–2 win in Game 7, and the fuzzy misfits of Oakland won their first of three consecutive world championships.

GAME 1	Oakland 3 at Cincinnati 2	GAME 5	Cincinnati 5 at Oakland 4
GAME 2	Oakland 2 at Cincinnati 1	GAME 6	Oakland 1 at Cincinnati 8
GAME 3	Cincinnati 1 at Oakland 0	GAME 7	Oakland 3 at Cincinnati 2
GAME 4	Cincinnati 2 at Oakland 3		

The Miracle Mets

America put a man on the moon in July 1969, but the most amazing event of the summer transpired in New York City. The Mets, who had never before finished above ninth place, overcame a 9½-game deficit, winning 22 of their last 27 games to claim the NL Eastern Division championship. Manager Gil Hodges's confident club, the Amazin's, led by Cy Young Award–winning pitcher Tom Seaver, swept Atlanta in the playoffs and upset a powerful Baltimore team in the World Series, winning in five. They were henceforth known as the Miracle Mets.

"I'm sure. I'm positive, I know there were people who changed their lives because of the Miracle Mets. People felt better. It was a good thing."

—Former Mets infielder Ed Charles

Nolan Ryan

Nolan Ryan was perhaps baseball's most beloved figure from the mid-'70s into the early '90s. His record 5,714 whiffs seems to be a mark that will stand indefinitely.

The "Ryan Express" captured 11 strikeout crowns with California, Houston, and Texas. His 383 punch-outs with the Angels in 1973 remain a major-league record.

Thanks to 20 seasons of double-digit victories throughout his 27-year major-league career, Nolan is tied for 15th on the all-time list with 324.

Ryan authored a record seven no-hitters (three more than anyone else), the last of which came at age 44.

W	L	ERA	G	CG	IP	H	ER	BB	SO
324	292	3.19	807	222	5,386	3,923	1,911	2,795	5,714

Ryan so overpowered Detroit during his no-hitter on July 15, 1973, that desperate slugger Norm Cash stepped to the plate carrying a piano leg.

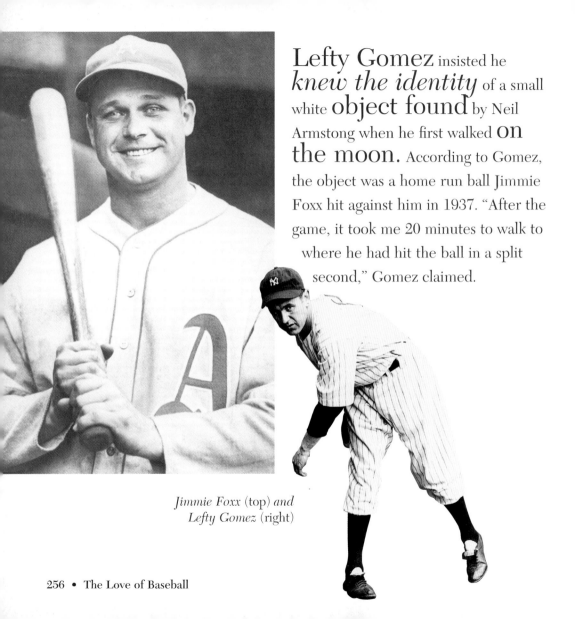

Lefty Gomez insisted he *knew the identity* of a small white **object found** by Neil Armstrong when he first walked **on the moon.** According to Gomez, the object was a home run ball Jimmie Foxx hit against him in 1937. "After the game, it took me 20 minutes to walk to where he had hit the ball in a split second," Gomez claimed.

Jimmie Foxx (top) *and Lefty Gomez* (right)

A 62nd-round draft pick
by the Dodgers, Mike
Piazza not only made the
majors but became the
greatest-hitting catcher of
all time. Through 2006,
he had ripped .300 nine
times, amassed 10 Silver
Slugger Awards, and
belted 419 home runs.

Fan or Fanatic?

Though rabid fans have always been part of the game, a few gained celebrity status in the '40s. One, a St. Louis rooter named Mary Ott, roamed the Sportsman's Park bleachers with a piercing laugh and booming voice described by one writer as "a neigh known to cause stampedes in Kansas City stockyards." That's particularly impressive when you consider Mary lived in St. Louis! The "Horse Lady of St. Louis" first came to national attention when revered umpire Bill Klem threatened to throw her out of a game in 1926.

Another prominent fan was Pete Adelis, who rooted for the A's. Believed to weigh more than 600 pounds, the "Iron Lung of Shibe Park" had a voice to match. He was even barred from the raucous Ebbets Field, though the Yankees hired him as a heckler against the Indians when they came to New York for a critical series in the '40s.

Connie Mack's Athletics had their own marathon man: Hyman Pearlstone made at least one road trip with the club for 44 straight seasons. George Doerzbach saw 55 consecutive Cleveland openers, and Atlantic City publicist Jimmie McCullough attended every World Series game for more than half a century, beginning in 1926. An AP dispatch described him as "the Babe Ruth of baseball fans."

CHAPTER SIX

Bringing It Home

"May the *sun never set* on American baseball."

—HARRY TRUMAN

What a Game!

July 13, 1896: Ed Delahanty cracks a single and legs out four inside-the-park home runs for the Philadelphia Phillies.

July 31, 1954: Joe Adcock blasts four homers and a double for Milwaukee against Brooklyn, needing only seven pitches to do it.

June 21, 1964: Jim Bunning throws a perfect game and doubles in two runs for the Philadelphia Phillies on Father's Day, humiliating the Mets 6–0.

May 8, 1968: Catfish Hunter tosses a perfect game for Oakland against Minnesota while cracking three hits and driving in three of the Athletics' four runs.

June 23, 1971: Rick Wise throws a no-hitter and slugs two home runs for Philadelphia against Cincinnati.

May 23, 2002: Shawn Green goes 6-for-6 with a double and four homers for Los Angeles, setting the major-league record for total bases in a game (19).

Catfish Hunter

Joe DiMaggio

He was the most regal of performers during his career with the New York Yankees, and the quiet, somewhat mysterious way he carried himself in later years only added to the legend of Joe DiMaggio.

Upon first coming to the Yankees in 1936, DiMaggio was no early candidate for nobility. This poor son of an Italian fisherman had what reporters called "squirrel teeth" and the naïveté to believe that a quote was some kind of soft drink. After hitting .323 with 44 doubles, 15 triples, 29 home runs, and 125 RBI his rookie season, he outdid even the great Lou Gehrig his second year, leading the league with 46 homers and 151 runs while batting .346.

Joe was a flawless ballplayer. A right-handed batter who almost always made contact—never striking out more than 39 times in a season—he was hampered by the 457-foot "Death Valley" in left-center field of Yankee Stadium but still managed to hit .315 there over his career. As a center fielder, he was fast and graceful but never flashy, making great plays look easy. Though quiet, he was a leader in the Yankee clubhouse.

After winning batting titles in 1939 (when his .381 mark earned him the MVP Award) and '40 (.352), DiMaggio captured the attention of the entire country in 1941. From May 15 to July 17, Joltin' Joe racked up a major-league-record 56-game hitting streak—during which he hit .408 with 15 homers. And if it hadn't been for two great stops by Cleveland's Ken Keltner, the streak would have stayed alive ... for who knows how long? The next day, Joe began another hitting streak, this one continuing for 17 games. He was the subject of songs, prompted contests and endless media coverage, and beat out Ted Williams (a .406 batter on the season) for his second MVP trophy.

> "Sometimes a fellow gets a little tired of writing about DiMaggio; a fellow thinks 'There must be another ballplayer worth mentioning.' But there isn't, really, not worth mentioning in the same breath as DiMaggio."
> —ALL-TIME-GREAT COLUMNIST RED SMITH

World War II intervened in 1943, and the 31-year-old DiMaggio came back three years later slightly below his previous form. His average and power numbers were down (he won a third MVP Award with subpar .315–20–97 totals in 1947), but he still had a flair for the dramatic. After missing the first 65 games of the '49 season with a heel injury, he returned to the lineup in Boston and hit four homers in three games—sparking the Yankees to the seventh of the nine world championships they would win in his 13-year career.

While his final statistics do not approach the all-time greats, when injuries and military service are factored in, Joe's average season translates into 34 homers, 143 RBI, and a .579 slugging percentage—numbers worthy of his 1969 selection by Major League Baseball as its "greatest living player."

BA	G	AB	R	H	2B	3B	HR	RBI	SB
.325	1,736	6,821	1,390	2,214	389	131	361	1,537	30

To prepare for his part as Grover Cleveland Alexander in the 1952 film
The Winning Team, *future president Ronald Reagan* (right) *worked*
with Indians ace Bob Lemon.

Mickey Mantle's
popularity stretched far and
wide, even as his career
waned. These youngsters
reach out for a touch of
greatness before the start of
a 1965 Yankees–Senators
exhibition game in San Juan.

Maz's *Series-winning* Smash

Game 7 of the 1960 World Series at Pittsburgh turned into a delirious roller-coaster ride. The Pirates went up 9–7 in the eighth inning thanks to a bad-hop grounder off Tony Kubek's throat and a Hal Smith three-run homer. But New York tied it up in the ninth in amazing fashion, forcing extra innings. Pittsburgh second baseman **Bill Mazeroski,** leading off in the bottom of the ninth, *smashed a climactic game-winning homer* that brought the players and Pittsburgh fans to their feet in celebration. Jubilant fans poured onto the field to celebrate the first World Series–ending homer in major-league history.

Notable Nicknames

Jittery Joe Berry

Don "The Weasel" Bessent

Ewell "The Whip" Blackwell

Downtown Ollie Brown

Pearce "What's the Use" Chiles

Nick "Old Tomato Face" Cullop

Willie "The Say Hey Kid" Mays

Fred "Crime Dog" McGriff

Julio "Whiplash" Navarro

Babe "The Sultan of Swat" Ruth - - - - -

George "Twinkletoes" Selkirk

Moe "The Rabbi of Swat" Solomon

Bill "Mumbles" Tremel

Walt "No-Neck" Williams - - - - -

Jimmy "The Toy Cannon" Wynn

Single-Season Home Run Leaders

1	Barry Bonds	73	2001
2	Mark McGwire	70	1998
3	Sammy Sosa	66	1998
4	Mark McGwire	65	1999
5	Sammy Sosa	64	2001
6	Sammy Sosa	63	1999
7	Roger Maris	61	1961
8	Babe Ruth	60	1927
9	Babe Ruth	59	1921
10	Jimmie Foxx	58	1932
	Hank Greenberg	58	1938
	Mark McGwire	58	1997
	Ryan Howard	58	2006

Barry Bonds

Long before Jackie Robinson broke baseball's color line in 1947, another talented young player survived a slew of racial epithets en route to a Hall of Fame career. Hank Greenberg, the greatest Jewish slugger in the game's history, still stands as baseball's sixth-best slugger with a .605 lifetime mark, and his career average of .92 RBI per game matches Lou Gehrig's 20th-century record.

1991: Twins vs. Braves

Minnesota and Atlanta were not even supposed to be in the World Series in 1991, as both had finished last in their respective divisions just the season before. Though a classic, this series was not noted for dramatic turnarounds or big comebacks. The two clubs just played each other about as deadly even as possible, and they did it for seven games.

There were weird plays, marathon games, unexpected heroes, creative baserunning, home-plate collisions, and dramatic homers. Kirby Puckett's stellar catch and 11th-inning, game-winning homer for Minnesota in Game 6 to stave off Series defeat was one of the greatest clutch performances of all time. In Game 7, Twins ace Jack Morris pitched a 10-inning shutout, and Minnesota won in the bottom of the 10th on a Gene Larkin single.

GAME 1	Atlanta 2 at Minnesota 5	GAME 5	Minnesota 5 at Atlanta 14
GAME 2	Atlanta 2 at Minnesota 3	GAME 6	Atlanta 3 at Minnesota 4 (11)
GAME 3	Minnesota 4 at Atlanta 5 (12)	GAME 7	Atlanta 0 at Minnesota 1 (10)
GAME 4	Minnesota 2 at Atlanta 3		

Carter *Clinches* It

After winning the 1992 World Series, the Toronto Blue Jays found themselves in a war with Philadelphia in the '93 fall classic. With their team down 6–5 in the bottom of the ninth of Game 6, Jays fans prayed for a rally to avoid a seventh game. With two on and one out, slugger Joe Carter worked the count to 2–2 on Mitch "Wild Thing" Williams—then crushed the next pitch over the left-field fence. After dancing around the bases, Carter was hoisted on the shoulders of his elated mates.

Unconventional A's owner Charlie Finley was a powerful, penurious,
and polarizing force during the '70s. On Opening Days, he forced his players to ride
onto the field on mules such as "Charlie O," the team mascot.

*Boston Red Sox Jimmy Piersall
lived the philosophy that playing
baseball should be fun. Armed
with a carefree attitude, Piersall
offset the pressures of baseball by
pulling more than a few zany
pranks. He circled the bases
backward after belting his 100th
home run. "That way I can see
where I've been," he said. "I
always know where I'm going."*

Stan Musial

A minor-league pitcher in 1940, Musial hurt his throwing arm diving to make a catch. Forced to the outfield when the injury failed to heal, he still made the majors the very next summer—and retired 22 years later as a .331 lifetime hitter with 475 homers, 1,951 RBI, and 3,630 hits.

Throughout the baseball world, Stan the Man was known as "an outstanding artist in his profession...a gentleman in every sense of the word."

Musial won seven NL batting titles and topped .300 17 times in his 22-year career. He was named the league's MVP three times (1943, '46, and '48) and was a 20-time All-Star.

"I believe the joy of getting paid as a man *to play a boy's game* kept me going longer than many other players."

—STAN MUSIAL

| | MAJOR LEAGUE TOTALS | | | | | | | | |
BA	G	AB	R	H	2B	3B	HR	RBI	SB
.331	3,026	10,972	1,949	3,630	725	177	475	1,951	78

PNC Park, Pittsburgh

With the emergence of many ballpark gems in recent years, ball fans and architects have struggled to decide which is best. ESPN and the Web site Ballparks of Baseball are among those who have picked Pittsburgh's PNC Park. The Roberto Clemente Bridge leads fans to an intimate ballpark with a panoramic view of the city's skyline. Features include statues of Pirate legends, baseball's most detailed scoreboard, and Manny Sanguillen's barbecue sandwiches. Delicious!

Hank Aaron

A glance at the lifetime stats of great players quickly shows the seasons in which they fell below what was expected; when they failed to deliver. Hank Aaron's stats, however, were consistently at the highest level. He slugged 20 home runs or more 20 seasons in a row. (The great Babe Ruth did it only 16 times.) He scored 100 runs in 13 consecutive seasons. And he tallied more than 100 RBI over and over again.

Aaron himself outlined the reason for the shape of his career. "Patience. It's something you pick up pretty naturally when you grow up black in Alabama. When you wait all your life for respect and equality and a seat in the front of the bus, it's nothing to wait a little longer for the slider inside."

At age 35, Aaron was considering retirement when historian Lee Allen sat him down for a chat. Allen pointed out that Henry was only a few home runs behind Mel Ott for the all-time National League record, and that Aaron stood a good chance to reach the 3,000-hit plateau as well as set the all-time record for at-bats. Aaron perked up. He realized he could quickly change the nature of his relatively silent career, and then he could use his reputation to make a difference in the situation of blacks in sports and throughout American life, as he stated in his autobiography, *I Had a Hammer*. Of course, Allen never mentioned Ruth's record of 714 lifetime homers. That record was untouchable, or so everyone at the time agreed.

So Henry kicked things up a notch, increasing his home run total from 29 in 1968 to 44 in '69. Then he hit 38, then 47 (the most he ever knocked in one season—and he was 37 years old!), followed by 34. The race to catch Ruth really began—a race against age, time, and bigotry. He withstood the pressure of a deluge of hate mail containing racial slurs and death threats, as well as a massive media blitz, and began a sensational finishing kick. In 1973, at age 39, Aaron slugged 40 homers—one in every 9.8 at-bats. He began the 1974 season just one behind the Babe.

Hate mail or not, Aaron was on a mission. He tied Ruth in his first plate appearance of the season. Two games later he walked in his first at-bat, then came around to score a run that broke Willie Mays's lifetime NL record. No one noticed. The next time he came to the plate, he used his magical wrists to loft an Al Downing pitch over the left-field fence in Atlanta. As he circled the bases, announcer Milo Hamilton shouted, "There's a new home run champion of all time, and it's Henry Aaron!"

With day-in, day-out consistent excellence over 20 years, Henry Aaron had pushed aside the unbreakable record. He finished his career two years later with 755 homers (a mark for the next guy to shoot for), 2,297 RBI (also a record), 3,771 hits (third all-time), and 2,174 runs—third all-time, and the same number accumulated by a guy named Ruth.

> "Trying to throw a fastball by Henry Aaron is like trying to sneak a sunrise past a rooster."
> —OPPOSING PITCHER CURT SIMMONS

BA	G	AB	R	H	2B	3B	HR	RBI	SB
.305	3,298	12,364	2,174	3,771	624	98	755	2,297	240

Fleet Feet

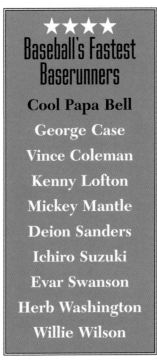

★ ★ ★ ★
Baseball's Fastest Baserunners

Cool Papa Bell
George Case
Vince Coleman
Kenny Lofton
Mickey Mantle
Deion Sanders
Ichiro Suzuki
Evar Swanson
Herb Washington
Willie Wilson

Satchel Paige said that Cool Papa Bell was so fast, he could turn off the light switch and be in bed before the room got dark. Another story goes that Bell swatted a ball *up the middle* but was out when it hit him before he could *slide into second.* The truth is he was simply amazing. Starring in the 1920s and '30s, Bell routinely scored from second on fly-outs or infield groundouts, and he claimed he once stole 175 bases in a 200-game season.

The effusive Sparky Anderson *(left, with Johnny Bench)* was a delight to be around, yet he demanded that his players follow a strict code of conduct. *"My way or the highway,"* he intoned. Anderson was the first skipper to win 100 games, world titles, and Manager of the Year Awards in both leagues (Cincinnati and Detroit).

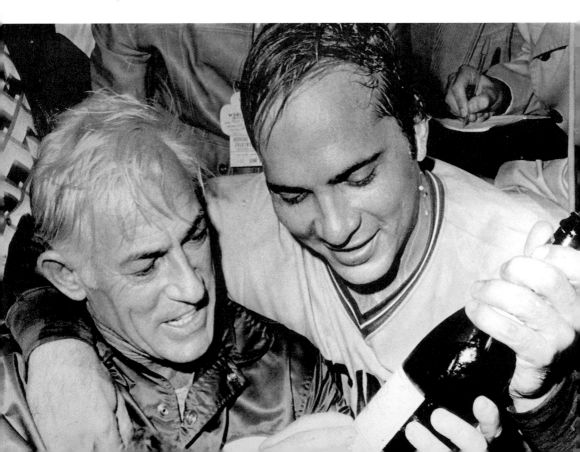

In April 1970, Brooks Robinson put a tag on his luggage that read "1970 World Champions." Six months later he was both a prophet and World Series MVP.

When he retired in 1980, **Willie McCovey** found himself in mighty good company: His 6.36 home run percentage was slightly better than Hank Aaron's, he ranked second in grand slams (18) behind Lou Gehrig (23), and his 521 career homers tied him with his boyhood idol, Ted Williams.

Glovework paved the way to the Hall of Fame for Ozzie Smith, "The Wizard of Oz," a 13-time Gold Glover.

Career RBI Leaders

1   Hank Aaron   2,297

2   Babe Ruth   2,213

3   Cap Anson   2,076

4   Lou Gehrig   1,995

5   Stan Musial   1,951

6   Ty Cobb   1,937

7   Barry Bonds   1,930

8   Jimmie Foxx   1,922

9   Eddie Murray   1,917

10   Willie Mays   1,903

Stan Musial

An estimated 200,000 San Franciscans welcomed the arrival of the Giants from New York on April 14, 1958. The next day, sluggers Willie Mays (left) and Hank Sauer (right) helped their club beat the Dodgers, 8–0, in the first game ever played on the West Coast.

A Family Affair

The odds that a human being will play in the major leagues are literally about one in a million. Yet those odds improve dramatically if one is a family member of a big-leaguer.

More than 100 major-league players raised sons who also appeared in The Show. As for siblings, more than 90 pairs of brothers have played on the same major-league team at the same time.

Hank and Tommie Aaron combined for more career home runs than any other brothers. Their total of 768 included just 13 by Tommie, a regular only as a rookie (1962). Joe Niekro hit his only major-league homer against brother Phil, beating him in a 1976 game. Together, the Niekros won more games (539) than any other pair of pitching brothers. Until Jason and Jeremy Giambi combined to hit 61 in 2002, the DiMaggios held the record for sibling home runs in a season. In 1937, Joe and Dom paired for 69, a total the DiMaggios matched in '41 with the help of 21 from eldest brother Vince.

The three Alou brothers—Felipe, Matty, and Jesus—batted in the same

Left to right: *Jesus, Matty, and Felipe Alou*

inning when the San Francisco Giants played the Mets at Shea Stadium in 1963. It was the only time in history three brothers batted for the same team in the same inning.

Barry Bonds (right) *and dad Bobby*

Three families have produced three generations of big-leaguers: the Bells, Hairstons, and Boones. Ray Boone, his son Bob, and grandsons Aaron and Bret Boone were all MLB All-Stars.

Late in the 1990 campaign, Ken Griffey, Sr., and Ken Griffey, Jr., became the first father–son tandem to play together. They started next to each other as the left and center fielders for the Mariners and also batted in succession—second and third in the order.

Griffey Sr. was then 40, twice his son's age, and in one game they both clubbed a home run. On October 4, 2001, Tim Raines, Sr., and Tim Raines, Jr., played in the same game for Baltimore.

However, no father–son duo has been more productive than the Bondses. Bobby's 332 big flys combined with Barry's 734 (through 2006) add up to a grand total of 1,066 round-trippers. Word has it that Barry's son, Nikolai, can hit a little, too.

Mike Schmidt

One of baseball's greatest power sources and a spectacular defenseman, Schmidt was named the starting third baseman on major-league baseball's All-Century Team.

The reliable fence-buster, who led the National League in homers a record eight times, holds the major-league record for home runs by a third sacker in a career (548).

Over his career, Schmidt earned three NL MVP Awards and 10 Gold Gloves (an NL record for a third baseman) and powered Philadelphia to the 1980 world title—their first title in 97 years.

Schmidt twice hit four consecutive home runs; Ralph Kiner is the only other man ever to do so.

BA	G	AB	R	H	2B	3B	HR	RBI	SB
.267	2,404	8,352	1,506	2,234	408	59	548	1,595	174

"I don't think I can get into my *deep inner thoughts* about hitting. It's like talking about religion."

—MIKE SCHMIDT

As a child in the
Dominican Republic,
**Pedro
Martinez**
sometimes played ball
with the head of his
sister's doll because
he couldn't afford
baseballs. Through
2006, Martinez
owned a record of
206–92 and boasted
the third-best
winning percentage
in major-league
history.

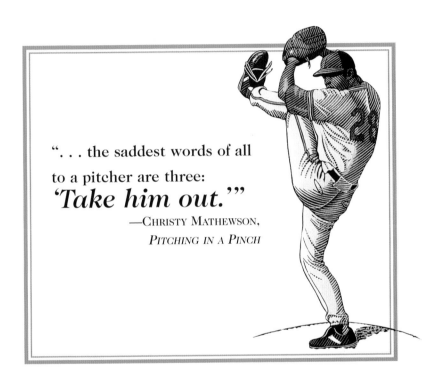

"... the saddest words of all
to a pitcher are three:
'Take him out.'"
—CHRISTY MATHEWSON,
PITCHING IN A PINCH

2001: Diamondbacks vs. Yankees

After mourning the September 11 tragedy for weeks, New Yorkers sought diversion in the World Series, as the Yankees aimed for their fourth straight world title. Fans sat back and watched a surreal fall classic that featured three of the most dramatic Series games ever played.

Down two games to one to Arizona, New York's Tino Martinez tied Game 4 on Halloween night with a two-out home run in the ninth. Yankee Derek Jeter clubbed a walk-off homer after midnight, earning the nickname "Mr. November." Incredibly, New York's Scott Brosius tied Game 5 with a two-out, ninth-inning homer, and the Yanks won in 12. But in Game 7, Arizona scored two in the bottom of the ninth to win 3–2, as Luis Gonzalez ended it with a bases-loaded single.

Lou Gehrig

Lou Gehrig's record of 2,130 consecutive games no longer stands, but what Gehrig accomplished in the seasons comprising his string remains a remarkable achievement. Only his own Yankee teammate, Babe  Ruth, can claim a more prodigious level of sustained offensive excellence.

Gehrig was a wise and modest man who drew far more solace from family than nightclubs. A native New Yorker and left-handed slugger at Columbia University, the sturdy six-footer joined the Yankees at age 20 in 1923 and saw limited duty behind star first baseman Wally Pipp for two seasons. The first game of Gehrig's streak came on May 31, 1925, when he entered the game as a pinch hitter. When he started the next day after Pipp complained of a headache, nobody thought much of it. In the end, Gehrig played the final 126 games of the season, finishing at .295 with 20 homers, and Pipp was out of a job.

Cleanup hitter on the Yankee pennant-winners of 1926, Lou paced the American League with 20 triples while adding 47 doubles, 16 homers, and 112 RBI. He also hit .348 in a World Series loss to St. Louis, but Ruth (who preceded him in the New York batting order) remained the main man with 47 homers and four more in the Series. "The Iron Horse" lessened the gap in '27, running neck and neck with Babe much of the season before finishing with 47 dingers. Although Ruth set the world afire by smashing a record 60 for the world champs, Gehrig won Most Valuable Player honors with astounding totals of 218 hits, a .373 average, 175 RBI, 52 doubles, 18 triples, and a .765 slugging percentage.

Lou upped his average to .374 in '28, leading the league with 47 doubles and 142 RBI. Similar stats followed each of the next nine years. Over 11 full seasons from 1927 to '37, Lou averaged .350 with 39 homers and 153 RBI (including an AL-record 184 in '31) while playing on five pennant-winners and four world champions. His numbers fell off to .295–29–114 when the Yanks took their third straight Series in '38, and some speculated that the streak was getting to him. In reality, the problem was a rare and incurable disease called amyotrophic lateral sclerosis—now known as Lou Gehrig's disease—that was slowly eating away at his body.

The suddenly sluggish and feeble-footed star took himself out of the lineup on May 2, 1939, and upon learning his fate shortly thereafter never played again. On July 4, 1939, as the Yankees saluted Gehrig in a sold-out tribute ceremony at Yankee Stadium, he told the hushed crowd that he had "an awful lot to live for." But less than two years later, he was dead at age 37—his 493 homers, 1,995 RBI, and .340 average a lasting testament to his greatness.

> "He was a symbol of indestructibility—a Gibraltar in cleats."
> —Sportswriter Jim Murray

BA	G	AB	R	H	2B	3B	HR	RBI	SB
.340	2,164	8,001	1,888	2,721	534	163	493	1,995	102

Iron Man II

After a players' strike ruined the 1994 season, Baltimore's Cal Ripken lured fans back to the game, winning them over on September 6, 1995. With President Bill Clinton and Vice President Al Gore in attendance, the classy Oriole played in his 2,131st consecutive game, eclipsing Lou Gehrig's "unbreakable" record. Ripken drove fans into a frenzy with a fourth-inning homer, then ran a "thank you" lap when the game became official after five innings.

The Homer in the Gloamin'

As darkness descended upon the friendly confines of Wrigley Field on September 28, 1938, hope for the beloved Cubs was still flickering in the twilight.

The Cubbies and Pirates were separated in the standings by half a game. The score was tied 5–5 in the bottom of the ninth inning with two outs. Had Pittsburgh managed to procure the third out, it was likely that the umpires would have called the game due to darkness, as it was already difficult for the batters to see the ball.

But as the last rays of sun disappeared and twilight wrapped itself around the park, Chicago's catcher-manager Gabby Hartnett launched a two-strike pitch into the left-field seats, securing a dramatic 6–5 win. The ecstatic crowd spilled onto the field and, along with the rest of the Cubs, joined Hartnett in a jubilant dash around the bases. The Cubs, who had trailed the Pirates by as many as nine games in August, had finally climbed into first place as the sun was setting over Wrigleyville, and Hartnett's long ball was thereby christened the Homer in the Gloamin'.

Inability to control his fearsome fastball kept **Johnny Vander Meer** out of the Hall of Fame. But when he was on, he was almost unhittable. In June 1938, Vander Meer, just 23 years old, became the only man in baseball history to pitch *consecutive no-hit games.*

Babe Ruth claimed the secret to his stroke—here analyzed in sequence by the publication *Mid-Week Pictorial*—was simply to swing his 54-ounce bat as hard as he could. *"I hit big or I miss big,"* he admitted.

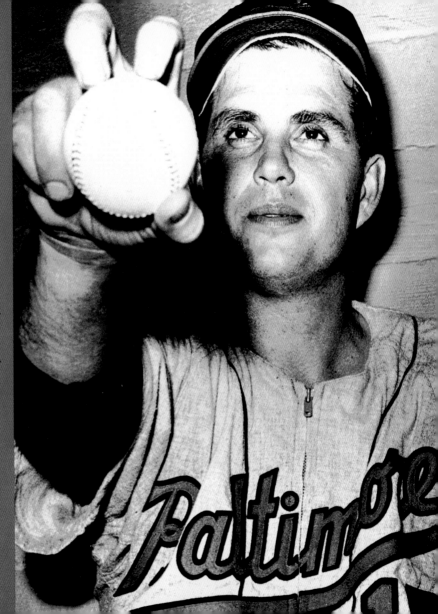

Hoyt Wilhelm's knuckleball—a pitch typically thrown with the fingertips—made him the first relief specialist elected to the Hall of Fame. In 1960, Orioles manager Paul Richards developed an oversize mitt so his catchers could snare it.

Connie Mack spent a record 50 seasons as manager of the Philadelphia Athletics. He was 88 when he finally retired.

Casey Stengel bids farewell to Yankee Stadium for the 1957 season
after his club dropped the World Series to the Braves. He returned to
the Series the next year, in another seven-game thriller, to win
a rematch with the boys from Milwaukee.

Reverse the Curse

Never before had a team clawed their way back from a 3–0 deficit to win a playoff series. But *the Boston Red Sox did it* in wild, exhilarating, unbelievable fashion in October 2004—and against whom? Their bitter rivals, the New York Yankees. With their backs to the wall, the BoSox reeled off a three-game win streak to even the series and then finished off the Yanks in decisive fashion. Star Johnny Damon swatted two home runs (one of them a grand slam) and drove in six runs in the seventh game, helping the team to a 10–3 victory. The Sox extended the streak to eight straight games, sweeping the St. Louis Cardinals to claim their first world title in 86 years. The *curse* Babe Ruth had supposedly laid on them had finally been *reversed.*

Index

O'Rourke, Jim, 32
Ortiz, David, 48
Ott, Mary, 258

P

Pabor, Charlie, 229
Paige, Satchel, 47, 91,
    170–171
Palmeiro, Rafael, 236
Palmer, Jim, 203
Parker, Dave, 49
Patterson, Arthur "Red," 14
Pearlstone, Hyman, 258
Perez, Tony, 30
Perry, Gaylord, 214
PETCO Park, 234–235
Piazza, Mike, 257
Pierre, Juan, 74
Piersall, Jimmy, 279
PNC Park, 282–283
Podres, Johnny, 192
Polhemus, Mark, 185
Pride of the Yankees, The.
    See *Movies, baseball.*
Prince, Bob, 40
Puckett, Kirby, 274
Pujols, Albert, 48

R

Raines, Tim, 99, 295
Raines, Tim Sr., 295

Reagan, Ronald, 266
Reardon, Jeff, 149
Reese, Pee Wee, 128
Reiser, Pete, 128
Richardson, Bobby, 216
Rickey, Branch, 36, 116, 191
Ripken, Cal Jr., 32, 49,
    304–305
Rivera, Mariano, 149, 178
Rizzuto, Phil, 74, 128
Robinson, Brooks, 32, 289
Robinson, Frank, 236, 247
Robinson, Jackie, 32, 36–37,
    116–117, 128, 191, 246,
    247
Rodgers, Bill, 81
Rodriguez, Alex, 142–143
Rodriguez, Aurelio, 124
Rodriguez, Ivan, 120
Roosevelt, Franklin Delano,
    15
Rose, Pete, 30, 84, 112,
    242–243
Ruth, Babe, 16–17, 18, 25,
    86, 87, 110–111, 113, 118,
    119, 192, 201, 208,
    232–233, 236, 271, 272,
    292, 302, 308
Ryan, Nolan, 158–159, 214,
    254–255

S

Sain, Johnny, 187
Sandberg, Ryne, 49
Sanders, Deion, 286
Sandlot, The. See *Movies,
    baseball.*
Sanford, Jack, 216
Sauer, Hank, 293
SBC Park, 150–151
Schmidt, Mike, 124,
    296–297
Scully, Vin, 40–41, 173
Seaver, Tom, 163, 214, 252
Selkirk, George, 271
Sherry, Norm, 27
Sierra, Ruben, 49
Simpson, Harry, 81
Sisler, George, 110–111, 166
Skizas, Lou, 229
Slagle, Jimmy, 185
Slaughter, Enos, 98
Smith, Hal, 268
Smith, Lee, 149, 178
Smith, Ozzie, 291
Smith, Red, 265
Smith, Wendell, 117
Snider, Duke, 146, 192
Snodgrass, Fred, 38
Solomon, Moe, 271
Sosa, Sammy, 7, 48, 49, 61,
    236, 272